W9-BVI-776

Job Satisfaction for Child and Youth Care Workers

Mark A. Krueger, Ph.D.

CHILD WELFARE LEAGUE OF AMERICA, INC.
440 First Street, NW, Suite 310, Washington, DC 20001

Current Printing (last digit)
10 9 8 7 6 5 4 3 2 1
Printed in the United States of America

Copyright © 1986
by the Child Welfare League of America, Inc.

CHILD WELFARE LEAGUE OF AMERICA
440 First Street, NW, Suite 310, Washington, DC, 20001-2085

ISBN# **0-87868-259-7**

CONTENTS

INTRODUCTION

The first edition of this book was written in 1980 with the intent of opening a discussion about what made child and youth care workers satisfied and productive. It was based on my experience as a worker and supervisor, and studies from child and youth care and related fields. Since that time I have been involved in three new studies and have documented more examples of the personal attributes, organizational factors and experiences that seem to contribute to workers' job satisfaction. This second edition summarizes what I have learned since the first book.

Job Satisfaction is usually defined as a worker's attitude about various aspects of the job, such as working conditions, supervision and administration, salary and benefits, opportunities to grow, and interactions with youth and colleagues. In other words, those workers who have positive feelings about these aspects of their jobs are generally more satisfied than those who have negative feelings.

There are many reasons why job satisfaction is important, but in child and youth care perhaps two reasons stand out more than the others. First, as shall be seen in the following chapters, there is mounting empirical and experiential support for the belief that higher levels of satisfaction are associated with lower levels of turnover and absentee-ism. Second, there is also growing support for the belief that satisfied workers are more effective workers. Hence, in a field in which permanency and proficiency are central to building relation-ships with troubled, difficult to treat youth, job satisfaction does indeed seem worthy of our atten-tion.

In this book we will look at some of the personal and organizational factors which seem to contrib-ute to greater satisfaction among workers. We will begin in Chapter One, WORKERS, by discussing the people who appear to be satisfied. This chapter includes a general profile of people currently working in the field, and specific descriptions of the various skills, attributes, thoughts and feelings of the pros: individuals who have the ability to work effectively with difficult youth over time and who seem to enjoy themselves in the process. In Chapter Two, ORGANIZATIONS, we will examine environmental or organizational factors (e.g., step plans, work schedules, supervision, and salaries), which seem to account for greater satisfaction. A method of proposing organizational change will also be discussed in this chapter.

Teamwork and team building will be the focus of Chapter Three, TEAMS. Here we will look at the structural ingredients and human conditions needed to implement satisfying and effective teams. The final chapter, CAREERS, is designed to help work-ers plan a meaningful, satisfying career in the field. Five career tracks and eleven career building steps are described in a way that will help integrate materials from previous chapters into individual plans of action.

Vignettes and examples are used each step of the way to highlight more didactic information. While an attempt has been made to weave some scientific facts into the narrative, this book is by no means a text or a technical manual on job satisfaction.

It is, instead, a collection of the "stuff" (approaches, programs, techniques, and personal attributes) which, based on my experience and study in child and youth care, seems to work. Readers are encouraged to examine the material, mull it over, build upon it whenever necessary, and then make their own decisions about what will work in their own job environment. Like our work with children, we have to learn as much as we can and then use what works, always keeping in mind that everyone has unique needs and each program or team its own unique philosophy.

CHAPTER ONE:
WORKERS

Jonathan is a youth care pro. For the past five years he's been coming to the Raintree Treatment Center with a smile on his face and tons of new ideas. Each day he enters the youth care office a few moments before starting time and eagerly maps out his shift. If there is a staffing or a team meeting, he attends and offers articulate insights about the youth. Afterwards he's off to the unit, problem solving, counseling, straightening-up, eating, playing a variety of games, designing projects, and finally, settling the group in for the night. Then he's ready to go home, a bit more tired perhaps, but enthusiastic about coming back the next day.

If you were to ask Jonathan's supervisor about him, he might say, "He's dependable, willing to change, always trying to grow, and he can really relate to the kids." If you could ask his co-workers, they might say, "We all like to work the same shift with him."

And if you could ask the director, he might say, "I wish we had a dozen more like him."

If Jonathan could be stripped of his modesty, he would probably admit that his commitment to and satisfaction with the work are what seem to distinguish him from some of the others. He might imply that somehow he's been able to face continuous struggles with very difficult to han-

dle youth and still enjoy himself in the process. He might also hint that he has learned from, rather than becoming embittered over, obstacles, such as having to deal with an insensitive public and trying to make ends meet from one month to the next. Then he would surely add that he loves the work, the kids, and his peers.

Jonathan represents, in simple terms, youth care pros: the people who seem to have the skills, intensity, stick-to-it-tive-ness, and desire to learn which are needed to work with troubled and/or handicapped youth. Students of the child and youth care field would undoubtedly agree that he is a "keeper": the type of person the field should be trying to attract and keep. Yet, if they were asked to be more specific, to describe in more detail the thoughts, feelings, attributes and characteristics of an effective, satisfied worker, they would struggle for an answer. One reason for their uncertainty would be that they simply have not talked about it very much. Another would be that effective workers are modest and, therefore, they are not prone to talk about themselves. And another, perhaps more significant reason, would be that effective youth work is a unique talent. One man's happiness and job skills are not necessarily another's. One woman's inspiration and energy may come from a completely different source than another's.

Nonetheless, the diffuse and individualized nature of the task does not diminish its importance. Like our attempts to describe the youth we work with, we have to do the best job we can and then hope others will embellish our observations. The purpose in this first chapter, therefore, is to make an attempt to draw a general profile of workers currently in the field and to discuss some of the additional characteristics, thoughts and feelings of "the pros," workers who seem to be both satisfied and effective in their work. The implied theme, then, will be that satisfaction and effectiveness, more often than not, go hand in hand.

A further intent is to provide a springboard for discussion among workers and administrators. For instance, workers can use this information to explore whether or not they have what it takes to sustain a satisfying career in the field. Administrators in turn can use this discussion to sharpen their recruiting procedures and to become more sensitive to the people who are doing the job.

Part of this discussion may at times seem a bit idealistic to some readers. If it is, it is because of the author's positive experience in the field and his fascination with people who seem to be able to meet the challenge: the youth work master craftsmen, scientists, and artists who not only stay, but are also capable of helping youth who others have long since abandoned. It is also reflective of the fact that the work requires very special people.

Other readers might think, "You can talk all you want about the workers, but unless agencies do more to keep them, what use is it?" If you are in this category, please be patient: the following chapters deal with crucial factors which promote the growth and development of youth care professionals.

A Profile

Perhaps the best way to start is to draw a general profile of the "modern" workers who will be addressed in this book. This will provide a launching point for the discussion in the next section of the special qualities that make many of them successful professionals. Most of the following information is based on two—1983 and 1985—international (U.S. and Canada) surveys of approximately 900 and 500 workers respectively from several states and three Canadian provinces (Krueger, Lauerman, Savicki, Parry and Powell, 1987). Both studies were conducted by the National Organization of Child Care Worker Associations in an attempt to better understand its membership and other individuals in the field.

Child and youth care workers work with troubled (emotionally disturbed, dependent/neglected, delinquent, etc.) and/or developmentally disabled children and youth in residential treatment centers, group homes, temporary shelters, correctional facilities, and community and home based programs. They spend most of their time in the "daily living environment" of the various facilities, but are increasingly called upon to work in homes and schools. Groupwork and "one to one" are still the most common methods of interaction with clients; however, many workers are also beginning to work with families. About 30% indicate that they have moved from a direct service position into an administrative, educational, supervisory or some other indirect service position. Most of them, approximately 85%, work on some form of treatment team.

Their average age is 32. They have been in the field about four years and at their current places of employment approximately two years. Of course many have been at their jobs much longer. Half are male and half are female. One-quarter are minorities. Approximately 70% hold a bach-

elor's degree. The most popular areas of study are social work, psychology, sociology, liberal arts and education. Almost one-third have completed or are working on a master's degree.

Their work weeks are normally 40 hours, but there are still some long shifts and overtime hours. For their work they are paid on the average between $13,000 and $13,999. A few are still paid as low as $8,000, but almost one-third are paid above $16,999. When asked if they would be in the field three years from now, two-thirds would reply yes.

From this general profile, four points of interest about the modern worker can be drawn in comparison to workers from previous years (Hylton, 1964; Krueger and Nardine, 1984; Myer, 1980; Rosenfeld, 1978; Wilson, Powell and Winer, 1977). First, these workers' overall level of pre-service education is higher; second, they are staying at their jobs and in the field slightly longer; third, the conditions in which they work have improved; and fourth, they are moving into administrative, educational, supervisory, etc., positions and maintaining their identity as child and youth care professionals. The significance of these differences will be addressed in the remaining sections of the book.

The Pros

We move now to a discussion of some of the specific feelings, thoughts, and skills which seem to be shared by the pros, people who have the ability to work effectively with youth over time and who seem to enjoy themselves in the process.

Most of the information presented here is based on the author's observations and experiences as a youth worker, and on discussions with hundreds of workers at training conferences throughout the U.S. and Canada.

They Have Twinkles in Their Eyes

John, a 16 year old youth, sits quietly on the couch in the living room of the group home. He is reading a copy of Sports Illustrated *while the other residents busy themselves with chores and table games. Rick, one of his youth workers for the past six months, enters the room, nods a friendly hello and then walks over and says, "What are you reading?"*

John casually looks up and responds, "SI. Sit down a minute, man. I want to show you something."

Rick accepts and John begins to explain how a story about Larry Bird, a basketball superstar, reminds him of a friend he used to play with on the playgrounds. As John speaks and points to pictures in the magazine, they lean closer to each other until their shoulders touch.

It almost goes without saying that effective youth workers are motivated by a strong affection for children or youth. Pros seem to be driven by the urge to reach a point where, as Al Trieschman once said, "The youth becomes a twinkle in your eye and you in his" (Trieschman, 1981). It is unthinkable that someone who didn't feel this way about youth could be very effective.

On the other hand, this rarely happens overnight. The "core of care,"—the compassion, trust, security and empathy—that is the foundation for any meaningful relationship takes time to develop, especially with youth who have been physically and psychologically abandoned throughout their lives (Maier, 1980). Hence, pros are aware that it will take awhile for most youth to "open up." They know it may take time and hundreds of positive interactions before an initial bond can be formed.

It is also undeniable that the chemistry is different with each child and that sometimes the proper mix can't be found. In other words, it is simply unrealistic to believe that all the youth will like you and vice versa. The key here for pros seems to lie in their ability to assess the significance of their relationships with each youth and to adjust their styles of intervention accordingly, always doing whatever is possible for every youth.

They Are Empathetic

> *Perry, the youthworker, looks quietly at Ken, 14, who is now lying face down on his bed after being physically restrained by Perry for almost fifteen minutes. Perry is frustrated and upset after being spit on, cursed at, and banged around. Yet he is trying to understand what's going on inside Ken; what possibly could have caused him to have a temper tantrum? He also asks himself how he might have felt in the same situation?*

Empathy, the ability to put oneself in other people's shoes, to see things from their perspective and to try to participate in their feelings and ideas, is perhaps the single most important quality of youthwork. Pros have the capacity to be empathetic. They may not always achieve their goal, but they are always trying.

7

They Like to Play

When the group is swimming, Mac, a 35 year-old youth worker, is in the water. When they are making papier-mache animals in the crafts room, he makes his own as well as helps the others. He pitches and catches in baseball, fishes on camping trips, and demonstrates all the gymnastics exercises. He also loves to play monopoly and bake cookies.

While the line, "Where else can you play and get paid for it" is often used with a bit of sarcasm, it is actually close to the mark in child care. Youth work is a good field for people who like to play and who can get enthused about trying new games and activities. In this context, pros are participators not observers. Adult-like in their capacity to understand the importance of play, they are child-like in their enthusiasm for being involved.

They Are In Shape

Maria, a youth worker for the last five years, jogs three times a week before coming to work. In the summer she bikes on weekends and in winter she cross country skis. She watches what she eats and she gets the proper amount of sleep. At work she is alert and usually very active.

There is little doubt that the work requires physical energy and stamina, perhaps more than any other human service profession. Pros seem acutely aware of this fact and consequently they seem to work hard at staying in good physical health. Barring uncontrollable illnesses or accidents, they usually have excellent work attendance records and they are able to maintain high levels of physical energy throughout their shifts and their careers.

They Individualize

Billy has been playing right field for the last hour and having little success either catching or hitting the ball. Josh, the youth worker, plays along, watching each player as best he can. Billy starts to get frustrated and begins teasing Rodney, the first baseman. At the end of the inning, Josh takes Billy aside for a few minutes and talks about his behavior. Once they are all together, Josh suggests that they play a game of kickball. The group agrees and in a few minutes everyone is having a good time. Billy in particular finds kicking and catching a larger ball more enjoyable and more suited to his skills.

Two youths are rarely at the same place in their emotional, cognitive and physical levels of development. Pros not only understand and accept this fact, they seem to have made it a paradigm for guiding their every action. For instance, they know that the way they must teach one youth to comb his hair, shoot baskets, rap with his peers and/or read may be miles apart from the way they must teach another youth. Hence, they must constantly challenge themselves to use individualized strategies and techniques, always striving to get to where the youths are, so that they can build strengths from that point.

They Have a Sense for the Group

Mary notices that three of the kids in her group are getting restless. They are off to the back of the rec. room slapping each other's hands and joking about something. Ordinarily this would not concern her very much, but these particular youth have gotten in trouble together before. So she walks over to the radio and turns it down, and then she goes over to the three boys and asks them to rejoin the others who are playing pool and ping pong. Once everyone in the group is in the same general area, she suggests that they all sit down and talk for awhile about the group's behavior and/or anything else they seem to have on their minds.

Managing difficult groups of troubled youth for extended periods of time is an extremely challenging task. Without a keen sense of group dynamics and a feel for both positive and negative group interactions, the task is nearly impossible. The pros seem to have a good intellectual grasp of groups and, perhaps more important, good instincts for when groups are going well or beginning to break down. It is almost as if they have antennae which constantly alert them to when someone is where they shouldn't be, when two or more members are about to form a counter productive sub-group, when noise levels are too high, and when horseplay is about to get out of hand.

Yet, while they understand the importance of structure and consistency in groups, they seem to never lose sight of the individual. They base their group activities and programs on the needs of each youth in their group, planning group activities and programs that meet as many individual needs as possible. They seem to avoid, whenever possible, group programs that remain static and expect all group members to strive for standards of behavior based on predetermined, generalized criteria.

They See the Systemic Nature of Problems and Solutions

"Sam doesn't deserve a home visit. His behavior here has been terrible all week," Louisa says at the weekly team meeting."

"Wait a minute. His behavior on the unit is only one factor. We have to consider how important it is for him to be involved with his family and his friends in the community. "They're part of the treatment plan too," responds Liz.

The notion that children can be treated in isolation from the familial, cultural and social systems of which they are a part has long since become passe. Yet circumstances and pressures in child and youth care often pull workers back toward one-tracked solutions which ignore the influence of systems outside the agency. Pros seem to have the capacity to resist this temptation, constantly reminding themselves and their colleagues that youths must be viewed as part of families, peer groups and cultures, and that whenever possible, individuals and elements from these systems must be involved in the treatment process.

They Believe It

At Harry's psychiatric consultation, Tim, the youth worker, says to the others (the therapist, the teacher, the psychologist, and his fellow workers), "We have to focus more attention on the daily living environment. There are some important relationships being developed there. Harry has also made progress on his grooming and privilege programs. Let's talk about this. I think it's pretty significant."

Convinced that important treatment takes place in their day-to-day interactions with youth, the pros advocate this position at staffings and in informal conversations. They seem to sense that while others may support this position, it is they who must believe in it and keep it fresh in the minds of their colleagues. At the same time, as team members they know that their importance is no more or less than other team members who feel equally strong about their own beliefs.

They Take Pride in It

Carl sweeps the hallway, whistling as he goes. Earlier he had cleaned the shorts of a youth who had soiled. Prior to that he had restrained a youth for almost an hour. It has not been the best of days and he is tired. Yet he feels good about having done his job.

There is a connection between every act performed in the daily living environment and treatment. Because pros seem to be able to see the connections, each aspect of their job is viewed as having a meaningful purpose. It is not surprising then that they seem to take great pride in performing what others might consider to be menial tasks.

They Vent and Problem Solve at Work

Bill had a rough shift, largely because he was left without double coverage. He had to remove a hefty 14 year old from the dining room because he was throwing food. He also had a runaway and he had to restrict the group from an outing because they were screwing around in the van.

Sensing that Bill could use a little support, two of his colleagues from another living unit invite him to join them for a few beers and a rap session after work. Bill is grateful for their offer, but he is leery about having a "late night" because he wants to get in to work early tomorrow and talk with his supervisor and teammates about his lousy day and express his anger about being left alone. He also knows that while "pub" discussions can be supportive, they can also lead to additional frustration if people don't follow

*through back at work. So he agrees to go, but
promises himself that he won't talk about people
who aren't there to defend themselves, and that
he will follow through the next day.*

Pros enjoy and use the support they get from
their colleagues after hours, but they also seem to
know that the real problem solving and venting
will have to take place in face to face contacts at
work. As difficult as it may be at times, they are
able to direct their frustrations and comments at
the appropriate colleague or supervisor.

They Are Open

*During a team meeting Bob says, "A few years
ago I experimented with marijuana. I'm no longer
using, but I want you all to know that I had a
problem, the same problem we are trying to help
the youth overcome. I want your advice about
how I should handle the issue when the kids ask
me about it."*

*"I'm glad you could tell us that, Bob," a fellow
worker says.*

*"Yes, I am too. I think it would be important
for you to share this with the kids, but only if
you now can say with conviction that drugs are
destructive and that you want to help them kick
their habits too," the team leader says.*

"I'm sure I can," Bob says.

Troubled youth seem to instinctively know when
someone is leveling with them or not. Effective
workers know this and they understand that they
must be open about their own beliefs, values and
problems if they expect the youth to do the same
with them. They also seem to realize that one of
the best ways to learn how to be open with youth

is to be open with fellow team members first (more on this in Chapter Three).

They Meet Their Needs Outside of Work

Kathy, a group home counselor, often spends her free time alone reading or listening to music or with a group of friends from college or with her boyfriend. She also enjoys hiking, going to movies and traveling. Most of her friends admire her for her ability to leave work behind and thoroughly enjoy herself.

As fulfilling as youth work can be, it will never be, nor should it be, a substitute for fulfilling relationships outside of work. Effective workers seem to be able to maintain a comfortable balance between the two. They enjoy their work most of the time, but they know that they must rely on their relationships and activities outside the agency as a primary source of support, comfort, and personal satisfaction.

They See Small Change as Big News"

Ken records with excitement the following changes in his log notes: "Willy combed his hair by himself." "Jack said hello today instead of the usual f..k you." "Tim and Burt played together for almost ten minutes without arguing." "Rich now has both wheels on his model roadster," and "Manny wore clean socks again."

Change, no matter how small, is constant in youth work. Pros know where to find it and they take great pleasure recognizing it.

They Are Articulate

Mary begins her report: Don, 14, is a troubled youngster who also has many strengths. Even though he has been abused and neglected by his parents, he still seems to have the capacity to relate well to others. For instance, he has a pleasant smile and a good sense of humor. He can also show affection, usually with a slap on the back, and when he is relaxed he seems to be a good listener, showing a sincere interest in what adults and peers are saying."

The ability to observe and report daily interactions is becoming increasingly important in child and youth care. Pressures from outside sources to be accountable, as well as the need to have accurate data for treatment decisions necessitate that practitioners constantly work at polishing their verbal and written communication skills. Pros are usually articulate or at least working very hard at developing the skills needed to communicate information to fellow team members and others, such as purchasers of service, judges, parents, administrators and local officials. They get pleasure and confidence from being able to share their observations in an understandable and useful fashion.

They are Eager to Learn

Liz has a bachelor's degree in education, but she looks upon it only as a foundation for her child and youth care career. Since coming to temporary shelter care two years ago, she has enrolled in a continuing education program in basic youth work and attended two regional conferences. She attends each in-service hour conducted by the agency and comes prepared with questions and information to share from the assigned readings. Next year she plans to begin work on a Master's Degree in Educational Psychology with a focus on youth work.

Child and youth care work is "high tech." Every year new techniques, strategies and theories are developed. The pros realize this. They see education as a continuous endeavor, an endeavor which is as much a part of their job as log notes, recreation periods, and team meetings.

They Are in Touch

Before he came to work, Art learned that he'd lost out on getting the apartment he wanted to rent. Then, as soon as he puts his foot on the unit, he finds Ricky's jacket and his baseball glove laying on a chair in the TV room. He rushes into Ricky's bedroom, grabs him by the arm and says, "Darn it, every time I start a shift, I find one of your things where it shouldn't be. I'm going to restrict you, maybe that will teach you..."

Ricky, completely surprised by Art's behavior, steps back and says, "But Art, I was just going in there to get it. We just finished our group meeting."

Art pauses a minute, looks at Ricky's confused face and says, "I'm sorry. I didn't mean to get on your case. I've got something else on my mind that's making me angry, but I'm not upset with you. Com'on, I'll walk you to the TV room."

Being in touch with one's own feelings, those which are brought to the job as well as those which are part of the job, is a vital prerequisite to helping youth understand their feelings. While getting in touch is perhaps one of the most difficult aspects of youth work, it can also be one of the most growth producing for the worker and the youth. Pros struggle with this, like everyone else, but they seem to work harder at knowing themselves. They are willing to explore their feelings

16

independently, with their colleagues, with the youth, and with their supervisors.

They Are Assertive

"I think we should cancel Tina's off-grounds for her poor school behavior," the team social worker says.

"I don't. There is no connection between the two. School behavior should be addressed in the classroom. If she needs to stay after to complete her work, fine. But why cancel her off-grounds? Especially now that she's doing so well in the community," Carrie, the youth worker responds.

Professional child and youth care workers are advocates for themselves and the youth. When the opportunity presents itself, they speak out, offer reasons for their objectives and present a different plan of action. They may not always win the day, but at least they "give it their best shot."

They Listen and Listen

Rod, the youth worker, begins to get a slight headache as he listens to Jason describe a field trip he's just gone on in school. This is the fifth rather labored account of the same trip Rod has listened to in the last hour. And there are still two other boys who want to share their adventures. So Rod is tired and a bit bored, but he smiles and nods his head as if Jason's account is both original and exciting.

There is nothing more reassuring to a troubled youngster than to know someone cares enough to listen. Yet, while listening is a fairly easy skill to develop, it is also perhaps the hardest to master. Pros seem to have found the secret, or at the very

17

least they understand the importance of listening and they try hard to listen as much as they can, even when they are tired and bored.

They Compromise

"O.K., I'm willing to go halfway on this. If Tom (age 14) can clean his room before school for another three days, then I'll consent to his being able to get up a little later," Sherry, the youth worker, says to her fellow teammates who have been trying to convince her that Tom doesn't need to continue getting up earlier in order to complete his chores. The others nod and they all move on to the next item on their busy agenda.

Compromise is at the center of consensus building and teamwork, two vital components of effective treatment decision-making and delivery. Pros know this and they constantly strive to understand where they can compromise on their own beliefs and values and where they can't. Whenever possible, they strive for consensus, but when they can't, they are clear about their reasons and willing to work at pursuing an alternative.

They Accept and Offer Criticism"

"When you get back so late with your group from the gym, there isn't enough time for them to shower and settle down for bed. That's why they're creating such a commotion and keeping the rest of the kids up," Louise says to Hal after stopping him in the hallway which connects her unit to his. "You're right about that. I should pay more attention to the time. Thanks," Hal responds.

Everyone can agree that constructive criticism is an important part of any work experience, but not everyone can give and take it. Pros seem to realize that criticism is a very important way to teach and learn, and they give it the same care and concern that they give to other aspects of team-work and communication.

They Are Career Minded

Steve wants to become a team leader in three years and then, if possible, move into the unit supervisor position. Erika wants to stay in direct service for about five years and then try to teach youth work at the local college. Pat wants to run his own program based on a child care model. Willy wants to be a practitioner for as long as possible. They are all members of the state association of workers.

Pros tend to view child and youth care as a life long endeavor. They are excited about being part of an emerging profession which has several career tracks, and they are able to take advantage of the situation by developing a personal career plan and by pursuing activities that will help them reach their goals. They are in it to stay. (More on this in Chapter Four.)

They Are Consistent

Roger asks his youth worker, Mary, if he can go into the poolroom by himself. "I've done all my chores and had a good day in school," he says.

"I'm sorry, Roger, but you haven't got that privilege yet. I'm very pleased with your behavior, but the team will have to review your progress and OK the poolroom before I can let you in there," Mary answers.

19

"Consistency, we need more consistency!" is a familiar battle cry in youth work. Team members and/or working partners learn very quickly that if they aren't consistent in carrying out their decisions, havoc can and probably will ensue. Pros understand this and never intentionally deviate from team decisions. Calculated risk taking, creative problem solving, and independent action are undertaken only when they are absolutely certain the situation requires it. In this context, they also feel comfortable saying, "I don't know. I'll have to check it out before I can give my approval." Consistency isn't always the simplest course, but over time it saves them and the youth from needless headaches and power struggles.

They Plan and Analyze

First thing Monday morning Hank pulls out his activity planner and fills it in with a variety of activities he hopes to conduct throughout the week. Included are activities for each individual group member, group activities and special subgroup activities. Friday evening, after the kids are sleeping, he goes over each activity in his mind and then writes a brief observation in his planning book: "Worked well, especially when the materials were laid out in advance." "Pete needs more work on his basic balance before we can use the balance beam again."

Organization and planning are often the only difference between a chaotic and a successful shift. The pros seem to have the extra discipline and enthusiasm it takes to be effective planners. They are able to build planning time into "their shift" with the same intensity that they put into their interactions with the kids. For them, planning indeed makes life easier and interactions more meaningful.

They Are Authoritative Disciplinarians

Jack, the youth worker, brings the group together for a discussion about their behavior in the van. He is concerned about the loud noises and general rustling around that occurred on their last outing. He wants the group to set a logical consequence for these behaviors before going on their next outing. He begins the meeting by saying, "I want to talk about how we can encourage each other to behave more appropriately in the van and then I want us to set a logical consequence in case the same behavior occurs again. But remember, I'll have to approve of any decisions we make."

Pros are AUTHORITATIVE as opposed to authoritarian or permissive disciplinarians. An authoritative disciplinarian encourages participation in discussions about discipline and explains his/her rationale for disciplinary actions. However, the underlying message is always that the adult is in charge and will do everything possible to maintain a safe, secure environment (Conger, 1980). This means, of course, that adults have final approval of all disciplines, even if they are in the minority. In contrast, permissive disciplinarians let the youth "do their own thing," and authoritarian disciplinarians take the approach, "You don't do it because I said so and that's it." Neither of these types of disciplinarians seem to survive for very long in youth work.

They Laugh a Lot

Robert, the youth worker, calls for the group's attention so he can demonstrate how important it is not to look down while walking on the balance beam. But as he turns to continue his demonstration he loses his own balance and stumbles onto the tumbling mat. Unhurt, he gets up and looks at the guys who are trying to hold in their smirks. As he's tucking in his shirt he bursts into laughter and they all follow suit.

A good sense of humor is essential for survival. If you can't laugh, then the job quickly becomes intolerable. Pros can laugh with the youth and at themselves. They like jokes done in good taste, and they find humor in simple day to day events that others often take far too seriously.

They Are Committed

During the interview process for her job, Carol was asked to give a two year commitment, which she did. However, prior to answering this request, she thought at length about what it would mean to her both professionally and personally. The interviewer, who is now her supervisor, had told her that the work would be tough and demanding, that the benefits were not great, and that he was in no position to guarantee that her position would be secure. But he'd also emphasized how important it was for the children to be surrounded with adults who they could count on to stay. So she knew that the job involved risk and hard work, but she also understood how important it was for her to be willing to see her commitment through. It wasn't an easy decision, but she made it with the confidence that she had thoroughly considered her options, including not taking the job.

Impermanence in relationships is often a fact of life for troubled and disabled children who have been psychologically and/or physically abandoned throughout their lives. Workers often add to this impermanence by leaving their jobs when things start to get rough or because they hadn't thoroughly analyzed their decision to take the job in the first place. Pros, on the other hand, understand the meaning of commitment. They know that they must make an initial investment in their job and strive to maintain that investment with intensity throughout their careers. The kids deserve nothing less.

Summary

In this chapter we have drawn a profile of child and youth care workers and explored some of the thoughts, feelings, skills, and attributes which seemed to be shared by pros. The intent has been to start by trying to identify the people who seem to be or have the potential to be effective and satisfied workers. If you have not already done so, it will be worthwhile to discuss with your colleagues additional observations and thoughts about this subject.

Chapter One References

Conger, J. (1979) *Adolescence and youth: Psychological development in a changing world.* New York: Harper and Row.

Hylton, L. (1964) *The residential treatment center: Children's programs and costs.* New York: Child Welfare League.

Krueger and Nardine. (1985) The Wisconsin child care worker survey. *Child Care Quarterly,* 13, (1).

Krueger, M., Lauerman, R., Grapham, M., and Powell, M. (1986) Characteristics and organizational commitment of child and youth care workers. *Child Care Quarterly,* 14, (1).

Krueger, M., Lauerman, R., Savicki, V., Parry, P., and Powell, N. (1987) Characteristics of child and youth care workers: A follow up survey. Forthcoming in *Journal of Child and Youth Care Work.*

Limer, W. (1977) Child care training needs assessment. Survey conducted by School of Social Welfare, State University of New York at Albany.

Linton, T. (1971) The educateur model: A theoretical monograph. *Journal of Special Education,* 5, (2).

Maier H. (1979) The core of care: Essential ingredients for children away from home. *Child Care Quarterly,* 8, (3), 161-173.

Myer, J. (1980) An exploratory nationwide survey of child care workers. *Child Care Quarterly,* 9, (1).

Rosenfeld, G. (1978) Turnover among child care workers. *Child Care Quarterly,* 8, (1).

Trieschman, A. (1981) *The Anger Within.* (A video tape series). Silver Spring Maryland: NAK Productions.

Trieschman, A., Whittaker, J., and Brendtro, L. (1969) *The other twenty-three hours.* New York: Aldine.

Wilson, T., Powell, N., and Winer, T. (1976) The Maryland Association of Child Care Workers' Survey. Unpublished.

CHAPTER TWO:
ORGANIZATIONS

For some reason workers stay longer at Pathways. And they don't just stay, they seem to grow together. No one is quite sure what makes Pathways different from many of the other centers which seem to have high rates of turnover and apathy among their staff. Observers and staff members have made what they think are some good guesses, but it is hard to put your finger on the one condition or combination of conditions that seem to create Pathways' positive atmosphere.

Various staff members have commented, "The pay isn't great, but it's above average." "We feel respected here." "They give you a chance to make some decisions." "The working schedules are tough, but reasonable." "If you work hard, you're pretty sure you'll be promoted." "Supervisors and workers support one another." "I like my team." "We have a good training program," and "They're straight with us about policy changes." But if you tried to determine which of these or other elements really accounted for Pathways' success, it would be extremely difficult. For each employee the reasons would probably be different, as would their definitions of the conditions they felt contributed to their growth and satisfaction. At this point, the leaders at Pathways are content to simply say "all of the above," and be grateful *that they have found a combination that seems to be working.*

Pathways has the type of atmosphere that many child and youth care administrators are trying to create: "a place where good people stay and grow." It is also representative of the "if it seems to work, use it" approach which most program developers have had to use to guide their attempts to remedy turnover and dissatisfaction among their workers. Without empirical evidence to rely on, they have had to use their practical judgment and general knowledge of human relationships to implement organizational practices which they believe have the best chances of succeeding. In some cases they have failed to find the right combination, but in others the results have been similar to Pathways'.

Now, fortunately, the field has also begun to study this very important area (Fleisher, 1985; Krueger, 1985; Krueger, Lauerman, Graham and Powell, 1986; Porter, Steers, Boulian and Mowday, 1974; Ross, 1984). These early studies are far from conclusive, but they are offering further support for some of the directions program administrators have already chosen and they are pointing to new directions.

Several of the organizational practices (e.g., recruitment, decision involvement, promotions, salaries, training, working schedules, and supervision) that appear to be gaining support will be described in this chapter. These are not foolproof practices, but they do seem consistent with available research findings and the recommendations of many individuals involved in child and youth care staff development.

The best way to use this information is for administrators and workers to discuss it together. Some of the practices may be familiar and others may be completely new. The objective is to adopt as many practices as are appropriate for your setting. This can be done with the confidence that all the practices described here have and are being implemented in other programs.

Recruitment

Jack, the supervisor, asks Mary, the candidate, to sit down; then he proceeds to outline the interviewing process. "First I'd like to tell you a little about our program. Then I want to ask you some questions about yourself and your views about working with youth. After that I'll try to be as honest as I can about the challenges and pressures you will face while working here. Next I'm going to ask you to go home so that we can both think about the interview. If we decide to move forward, I'll invite you back to meet the children and to be interviewed by some other people, including those folks who you'd be likely to work with. If you are hired we have a six month probationary and training period to give us both time to decide whether or not we want to have a long-term relationship."

Getting the right people is obviously the best place for an organization to start. This is not a simple task, but it's worth the effort to develop an extensive recruitment process. Crisis or "reflex" hiring (sometimes jokingly referred to as "taking warm bodies off the streets") invariably leads to disaster. An agency might luck out now and then, but usually hasty selections lead to agencies full of apathetic, dissatisfied employees. On the other hand, agencies that work hard at finding people who will fit into their long range plans seem to have much more success in finding and keeping people who can grow within their organization. Following are a few general suggestions which are becoming informal rules for effective recruitment.

Look in the Right Places

College recruitment offices, local and minority newspapers, and child and youth care journals are good places to leave job announcements. Another excellent place to advertise is with fellow recruiters. For example, it is helpful to set up a network among local child and youth care supervisors. Often supervisors will have two or three good candidates for one position. Why not refer the ones that aren't hired to another supervisor?

Screen Applications

Careful screening is important. There are no secrets to this other than being sure that the application has the types of questions that will legally help you identify people who could potentially fit the bill. Detailed attention should be paid to the answers written on the application before setting up an interview. It helps to have two or more people screening the same applications to identify preferred candidates. Some interviewers develop a rating system to help sort applications. Rating scales are a good idea as long as all raters feel comfortable with the measures used and that everyone involved uses the same criteria. It is also important to make sure that your criteria do not illegally discriminate.

A few general factors to look for include education, experience, track record, special interests, and references. A bachelor's degree in human services is increasingly becoming an entry level requirement—not because a formal learning experience guarantees a better candidate, but because there are so many applicants with bachelors' degrees and because many of them also have some related experience, either in a field placement or in part-time jobs held while attending school. In other words, if you can get educated people with related experience and the necessary personality characteristics to do the job, this is a better combination than having people with only experience and characteristics. Professional child care requires good academic skills (writing, reading, etc.) and is enhanced by a basic knowledge of topics such as human development, counseling, parenting, family work, behavior mangement, etc. which are part of the curriculum of many undergraduate programs. With the development of dozens of new college programs over the past ten years, there are also an increasing number of candidates with undergraduate specialties in child and youth care (Vander Ven, 1986).

Special interests or areas of academic concentration that correlate with types of things children like to do (e.g., art, music, recreation, vocational training, etc.) are also important to look for. Gaps in special programming can often be filled by bringing in people with the necessary expertise as child care workers as opposed to hiring specialists. (For example, instead of hiring an athletic director, hire a youth worker with experience in athletic programming.) This idea will be discussed further in the section on Step Plans.

If your candidate has experience, look to see if the name of his or her supervisor is among the list of references. Applicants who avoid using a former supervisor have often left previous jobs under duress or unfavorable conditions. This may or may not create problems, but it should be looked into.

Inform

The initial interview can begin with an outline of the interviewing process, followed by an overview of the opportunities in the field (see Chapter Four), and an explanation of the agency philosophy. Candidates for child and youth care jobs often come to the interview blind—not because of shortcomings on their part, but because little is known outside the agency about the worker's role within the agency. Even candidates with related experiences may not know much about your specific program. Therefore, in order to make an informed decision, they will need as much information as possible about the program.

Look for the Right Characteristics

In the first chapter, characteristics of effective workers were discussed, so we need not repeat them here. However, it is important to emphasize that you have to know what you're looking for in order to get it.

One suggestion is to frame a question around each of the characteristics and attributes outlined in Chapter One. For example, ask questions such as, "How do you feel about children?" "Do you consider yourself to be very active?" "What are some of your special interests?" "Are you able to accept criticism?". . .

Get to Know the Candidate

Try to find out as much as you can about the candidates' own upbringing and their beliefs and values regarding the problems they will encounter, such as chemical dependency, emotional illness, sexual abuse, etc. The objective is to determine areas of compatibility and, especially, incompatibility. Questions might include, "What is your treatment philosophy regarding sexual abuse, drugs," etc. "Tell me a little about what your childhood was like?" "How do you feel about alcohol and drugs?" "Do you use either?" "Have you ever been abused or do you know someone who was?" "How do you feel about abuse?"

No one is very happy for very long in an environment where their values and beliefs are constantly in conflict with the program philosophy. Therefore, it is important to learn as much about a candidate's experiences and views on important issues as soon as possible. Final decisions about whether or not a candidate is compatible should always be made by consensus among interviewers. It is simply too difficult for one person to make a determination alone. If a person appears incompatible it is important to explore issues further with him or her and, if possible, reach a mutual agreement that your agency may not be the best place for that person to work. At no point, however, do you want to give the impression that the candidiate's different views on the issues are less valuable or moral than those of you or your agency.

Test

Some recruiters use psychological testing to help learn more about their candidates and this seems to be a positive step. Tests in combination with interviewers' assessments and instincts can offer valuable information that may not have been revealed in the interview alone.

Be Up Front

Before the candidate leaves, be honest about the demands and benefits (or lack thereof) associated with the job. Being up front about these issues eliminates misunderstandings later. Besides, if you can discourage a candidate in the interviewing process, it is unlikely that they could have survived the first few months anyway. Ask candidates to go home and think about the interview and about whether or not they could make a commitment should they be offered a job.

Conduct Several Interviews

If a decision is made to bring a candidate back, always have at least one other administrator and as many of the potential teammates as possible involved in further interviews. It is also helpful to have the children meet a candidate (if he or she looks promising) and to have the person spend some time with the staff and children "on the unit." Then make a joint decision and begin the probationary period.

Commitments

"Jack, I'd like to offer you the job, but before I do, I want you to think for a few days about whether you can give us at least a two-year commitment. I've tried to be honest about what you're going to encounter here and we'll try to do every-

thing we can to make it a meaningful experience for you, even though we can't guarantee your job for two years. Don't get me wrong, we'll do every-thing possible to make it work, but we feel it is important that new employees come into the job willing to give the kids at least two years. Please think very carefully about the pressures and demands you'll face before you give me an answer."

It is fair to expect commitments from new employees as long as the agency is committed to holding up its end of the bargain. Sometimes it doesn't work out, but both parties must begin with firm commitments of at least two years. It takes that long in some cases for new workers to adjust to the job and to provide the kind of program stability that youth need. Even if the youth only stay for a few months, they need to know that those who care for them are committed, both to the agency and to the youths it serves. A stable organizational environment is equally important to short and long term programs.

Decision Involvement

Staff members at Hilldale have many oppor-tunities to become involved in decision-making. As team members, they are largely responsible for developing individual treatment plans for their group. They also attend full staff meetings and participate in major policy making deci-sions for the agency. Then, of course, there are the autonomous decisions they must try to make "on their feet" each day as they interact with the kids. Some of the decisions are pretty tough, but they enjoy the challenge. No one wants to go back

*to the old days when most of the decisions were
made for them by administrators and clinicians.*

In one study of workers, their perceived level
of decision involvement was the second strongest
predictor of their satisfaction and commitment to
their agencies (Krueger, 1985). This is consistent
with the popular participative management theory
which suggests that employees are likely to feel
better about their work and to be effective if they
have a strong voice in operating the "plant" (Katz
and Kahn, 1978). Hence, without further elabo-
ration at this point, it seems clear that it is bene-
ficial for agencies to open as many doors for decision involvement as possible. (More on this topic
in Chapter Three under "Teams.")

STEP PLANS

*Rick has been with the agency for two years.
He is currently working very hard on becoming
a Youth Worker III. If he makes it, he will be
eligible to move into a higher salary range and
he will assume some leadership responsibilities
on his working shift. In order to make it, he's
going to have to complete the youth work course
at the U., get certified by the child care association, finish work on a special recreation project
he's setting up for the kids, and maintain a consistent level of daily performance.*

Step plans are systems which make it possible
to be promoted within the ranks, to take on additional responsibilities and to receive additional
incentives without having to move from direct
line work (e.g., Youth Worker I, Youth Worker II,
Youth Worker III...). In recent years, support for

step plans has grown considerably. Like decision involvement, step plans were also one of six predictors of satisfaction (Krueger, 1985). Fleischer (1985) also included "career pathing steps for promotions" in her recommendations for reducing turnover. Program developers also appear to believe that having a chance to grow, to take on additional responsibilities, and to be promoted are important program assets. In the two cited international surveys of workers, approximately 50% of the workers said they worked in agencies with some form of step plan (Krueger, et al., 1986; Krueger, et al., 1987).

A SAMPLE: Following is a very basic sample of a three level step plan. Most step plans are far more detailed than this one. The objective here is merely to provide a feel for "how the system works." (Salaries reflect realistic 1986 levels.)

Youth Worker I:

QUALIFICATIONS: College graduate in human services (child/youth care preferred). Exceptions can be made for experience (two years) if the applicant is highly recommended and plans on continuing his or her education.

SALARY: $14,000-$14,999.

RATIONALE: This is an introductory position for new workers. The average time in this position should be one year.

Requirements:

—Satisfactorily completes the introductory inservice.
—Follows procedures in child care manual.
—Is dependable and timely with assignments.

—Works with and follows instructions of person in charge of shift.
—Is willing to help with other groups.
—Is flexible in responding to scheduling needs.
—Dispenses medical supplies and prescriptions according to procedure.
—Completes first aid course.
—Contributes to development of individual treatment plans.
—Tries to consistently carry out treatment decisions.
—Comes prepared to supervisory conferences.
—Plans appropriate group activities.
—Writes objective logs and reports.
—Cooperates with team members and other agency staff.
—Participates in training.

Youth Worker II:

QUALIFICATIONS: At least one year experience at the agency in which the candidate has demonstrated the ability to follow YWI specs.

SALARY: $15,000 to $16,999.

RATIONALE: The nucleus of the youth work staff will fall in this category. These are workers who have proven themselves in their first year and who are constantly striving to expand their horizons and polish their skills. Many of these people will eventually be candidates for Youth Worker III positions.

Requirements:

—Continues to meet basic YWI requirements.
—Continues to build relationships with team members and takes an increasingly active role in treatment planning.

—Is able to adjust to the physical and emotional demands of the job.
—Actively pursues new information pertaining to own personal growth and program development.
—Initiates special events and special groups such as group outings and recreational activities.
—Is ready to step in for the person in charge of a shift if that person is ill or drawn away by a crisis.
—Displays a positive working attitude and is willing to help new workers.
—Attends at least 20 hours of outside workshops in addition to 40 hours of in-service training.

Youth Worker III:

QUALIFICATIONS: A minimum of two years experience at the agency in which the candidate has demonstrated an exceptional ability to meet YWII specs. Professional certification.

SALARY: $17,000+.

RATIONALE: This is a leadership, teaching and/ or semi-supervisory position. People promoted to this position have proven that they have special qualities that will help in overall staff development and they have demonstrated a strong commitment to the agency and their work.

Requirements:

—Continues to demonstrate exceptional ability to meet YWII requirements.
—Assumes leadership of treatment team if designated.
—Assumes charge of working shift if designated.

—Assumes educational and leadership responsibilities for a program specialty area if so designated.
—Works hand in hand with head supervisor to provide support and problem solving alternatives to Youth Worker Is and IIs.
—Participates in selection of new staff when so designated.
—Promotes the agency in the community.
—Participates in 30 hours of outside training in addition to 40 hours of in-service.

Following are a few tips for developing step plans:

Involve Staff Members in Setting up the Plan:

The best way to identify meaningful criteria for advancement and incentives is to involve the staff in the process. Staff members can list the skills, knowledge areas, and personal attributes which they feel are needed at certain levels of performance. They can also list the types of incentives (e.g., salary, working shifts, decision-making) which are most meaningful. Then, with this information at hand, the administrator can draft several alternative plans which staff members can discuss and vote on.

Develop a Cadre of Top Workers:

One of the major goals for a step plan is to create "top slots" for the workers who can serve as models for the newer, less experienced staff. New workers will learn more from experienced workers than from anyone else in the agency. If the experienced workers are productive and enthusiastic, then new workers are likely to be the same. On the other hand, nonproductive, apathetic, senior workers tend to "burn out" new workers very quickly.

Have Several Ways to Advance:

Developing leadership skills is one of the major purposes of step plans. It is important to have people who can assist supervisors by being leaders of working shifts and treatment teams. Step plans, however, can also promote the development of skills in specialty areas such as music, art, recreation, special events, evaluation, etc. For example, in some step plans workers can advance from one level to the next by displaying the skill to train or develop programs in one of these areas. This pays off by reducing the need to bring in outside specialists. Hiring people with specialty backgrounds as child or youth care workers also helps in this regard.

Opt for Promotions:

When there are very limited financial resources available, tough choices about who should get them have to be made. It is better, however, to make resources available to those people who are doing the job than to those who aren't or who haven't learned how yet. This means that it may be wiser to give a larger percentage of the total annual salary allotment to workers who are advancing in the step system, as opposed to raising starting salaries or raising salaries across the board. It also means that some workers may have to be "frozen" at a certain point. No one should remain frozen for very long, however. Workers who aren't motivated by the second evaluation can be encouraged or asked to move on. Many agencies are overidden with employees who are content to keep doing things the same way day in and day out, never challenging themselves to grow.

Offer Several Incentives:

Salary increases are, of course, very rewarding to most child and youth care workers. However, the opportunity to work certain shifts, to gain greater decision-making autonomy, to teach and supervise peers, and to learn should never be underestimated. Whenever these additional incentives can be integrated into a step plan, it will be more meaningful to most of the participants.

Include Outside Training and Certification:

In addition to performing on the job, criteria for advancement can include courses, workshops, and certification offered by the professional child care community. Training is available from many sources (e.g., colleges, professional associations, conferences, private training groups, etc.) and certification is available in many states. It is difficult to be an effective professional without an awareness of the body of knowledge being developed outside the agency.

Salaries

Mary has to live with two other women in order to make rent. Bob can't afford to get his used car fixed again and he certainly can't buy a new one. Nick's wife wants to stop working so they can have a family, but it would be impossible unless Nick changed jobs. Nancy can't remember the last time she went out to a nice restaurant and a show in the same evening. Hank's wardrobe is down to two pairs of jeans and three or four shirts. Terri would like to return to school but there is no way she can afford the tuition.

Whereas salary may not be as important as some other variables in terms of contributing to an employee's long term job satisfaction, it is very important over the short run, especially when the worker is having a hard time meeting basic needs. When workers can't afford to live alone or have a family when they want to, when they can't afford decent transportation to work, and when they must dress and eat at near poverty levels, something is wrong. Unfortunately this is the case for a large number of workers who fall into average or below average child and youth care salary ranges (current average range is approximately $13,000 to 13,999).

On the other hand, some administrators feel that it is worth the effort to at least draw workers salaries closer to or in line with salaries paid for members of other disciplines with similar backgrounds. For instance, in these agencies, teachers, social workers, and child and youth care workers with bachelor's degrees are paid the same. This accomplishes three goals. First, it raises salaries slightly. Second, it gives workers the feeling that they are indeed worthy of the same status as other people with similar experiential and educational backgrounds. Finally, it increases the probability that workers will stay longer, provided that the agency follows the other practices presented in this chapter.

The major question is usually "Where will the money come from?" This is a legitimate question, especially in a field where there seems to be a constant shortage of funds. It is worthwhile to note, however, that there seems to be little correlation between what comes in and what goes out to workers. For example, the highest paid workers do not necessarily work in the agencies that receive the highest fees for their services. How can this be? The administrators in some agencies have made a commitment to child and youth care and found creative ways to give them a more equitable piece of the salary pie.

Workers Supervising Workers

Dan was a youth worker for five years before he became a supervisor and he is very glad he was. His experience has helped him be a more effective model for his staff and has given him sensitivity and insight which couldn't have been gotten any other way. For instance, he has a good feel for when staff members need him to be present and when they don't. He also feels that he can understand some of their frustrations and that he knows what to expect when he wants them to take on additional responsibilities. The education he received while working on his master's in Educational Psychology was helpful too, but he is convinced that "there is no substitute for experience."

Experience on the front line is a valuable asset for supervisors and leaders of child care staff. It helps them be more empathic and aware of the needs of their staff members. They need formal education as well, but formal education alone is usually not adequate, nor is supervisory experience in another profession.

Filling these positions "from the ranks" also promotes career development and gives workers the message that they are valued as professionals on par with other professionals within the agency. Administrators who are prone to hiring social workers or teachers as child or youth care supervisors can ask themselves the question: Would I hire a child or youth care worker to supervise my social work or education staff? If the answer is no, then they will have a better understanding of how strongly most child and youth care professionals feel about being supervised by their colleagues.

Schedules

The child care supervisor begins the weekly child care meeting with, "In front of you is a blank copy of the monthly schedule. If you like, you can use it to develop a new working schedule. I'm going to give everyone on the staff two weeks to get their proposals in to me. Then we'll all sit down and try to work out a new schedule together. As you're developing your proposal, keep two goals in mind. First, we want to have a schedule that provides the best possible coverage for the kids, and second, we want to try to meet as many of our own personal needs as possible."

Most workers like their odd working hours, which often include a combination of weekends, days and nights; otherwise they would have taken jobs that follow the "nine to five" routine followed by many of their friends. Their schedules can become very taxing, though, if they are filled with overtime and if they interfere constantly with the their personal lives. To avoid this, there are two rules of thumb to follow. First, keep overtime to a minimum. Forty hours is plenty of time to spend with groups of troubled youth; any additional time should be spread thinly and evenly among staff. Second, involve the workers in the schedule making process. Even if they don't get what they want, workers tend to be more satisfied with schedules that they have had a part in developing. They are also often very adept at recognizing how schedules can be adjusted to meet more of the youths' treatment needs and, in most cases, are willing to go the "extra scheduled mile" in order to accomplish their goals.

Introductory Training

Jack, the supervisor, walks Bob, the new recruit, to the youth worker office where Tina, a YWIII, is waiting to meet them. After they enter, Jack says, "Bob, this is Tina. She'll be working with you for the next two weeks. She is one of our most experienced workers. I want you to stay close by her side and remember, no question is too dumb to ask. I'll be back to get you later in the day so we can review what's happened. I'll also be explaining the rest of our training program to you at that time. Good luck."

Getting off to a good start has a tremendous impact on a new worker. The initial attitudes and working conditions a new employee is exposed to can set the direction and tone for everything that follows. "Being thrown to the wolves," or "having to learn entirely by trial and error," often leads to permanent dissatisfaction. On the other hand, satisfied workers can often recall the support and encouragement they got from the supervisor and their colleagues during the very difficult first few weeks or months on the job.

An effective introductory in-service program usually includes the following elements:

Time to Work Alongside a Pro:

Being able to work alongside a professional experienced worker for at least two weeks without having direct responsibility for the youth is a must. As mentioned previously, workers generally learn more from their colleagues than anyone else. Therefore, initial modeling of enthusiastic, effective youth work is very important, as is having the security of knowing that help and support are always at hand.

Regular Contact with the Supervisor:

Daily or regular contact with the person in charge is also vital. Supervisors can help answer questions, clarify misunderstandings, and provide additional support. If only for a few moments on some days, it is important for new workers to know that they have regular access to management.

Forty Hours over Six Months:

At least forty hours of formal introductory training are needed. This training, however, does not have to be crammed into the first few weeks. As a matter of fact, it may be better to spread it out over six months. Giving new workers too much too soon adds pressure which most of them do not need as they're trying to learn how to cope with the children and adjust to new working schedules.

Topics Covered:

The topics covered in formal training sessions usually include basic material such as daily operating procedures, treatment philosophy, behavior management techniques, self awareness, emergency procedures, first aid and the like.

Individual Pacing:

Each new worker is able to assume responsibility for the youth at a different pace. Some can handle "the group" rather quickly and others may take more time. This is not an indication that one worker is better or worse than another. It is simply a reflection of different abilities. Therefore, whenever possible new workers should be given the reins at a pace which is consistent with their ability to handle them. Many of the best workers in the field have emerged after having considerable difficulty at the beginning.

Constant Feedback:

New workers need to know how they're doing. The more feedback they can get from their colleagues and their supervisor, the more likely they are to grow.

Supportive Supervision

Jeff knows that he will receive one hour of individual supervision from Sherry every week come rain or shine. In the two years he's been with the agency, he can only remember having supervision cancelled a couple times. When his friend Jerry, who works at another agency, asked him how they pulled it off—Jerry could only remember meeting a few times with his supervisor over the past six months—Jeff said, "I'm not sure? I think it's because we both think it is very important. I look forward to those meetings. I always come away charged up for another week. Maybe she feels the same way. We have team supervision too—every other week."

There is little doubt among professionals that supervision is essential to worker stability and growth. For example, Fleicsher (1985) found that "supervision" or lack thereof was a major reason why workers left their agencies. She concluded that increased monitoring of supervisory effectiveness and supervisory training were essential strategies for reducing turnover. Workers need and deserve support from supervisors the same way that children need and deserve their support. Following are a few supervisory guidelines:

One Hour a Week:

One hour of individual supervision a week has been an accepted goal in professional child and youth care for years; however, it also seems to be one of the toughest goals to reach. Something always seems to be ready to impinge on supervision (a crisis with the kids, a shortage of coverage, the supervisor is called away, etc.) and it usually will if the supervisor and the supervisee let it. The only way to get supervision on a regular schedule is to make it a priority. Missing supervision should be akin to missing work.

A Time for Growth

Effective supervision is a time for positive feedback, teaching, identifying and solving problems, reviewing goals and objectives, planning careers, and discussing strategies and techniques. Workers usually leave these sessions having learned more about their own strengths and weaknesses, having learned new approaches for working with kids and solving problems, and feeling rejuvenated for another week.

Time to Plan

Each youth worker at the group home is given approximately one hour of planning time each day. This time is used to review logs, fill out activity planners, write consultations...

Youth work requires as much planning and preparation as social work, education, or any other human service endeavor. Workers can't be successful if they are expected to "wing it" all the time. Unprepared workers tend to be frustrated, reactive workers, whereas prepared workers tend to be more confident, preventive and supportive.

Keep Workers Informed About Internal and External Policies

At the full staff meeting, Martin, the executive director says, "We've just received the new budgets which are based on the six percent increase proposed by the state. I want to go over these with you today. I also want to share some information I've gotten about future trends in placement of children. Then I'd like to hear your opinions and recommendations."

Workers who are aware of and have a part in major policy changes are bound to be more effective. They are also more likely to be sensitive to the pressures faced by top administrators. Keeping workers in the dark about these issues generally serves no purpose other than promoting mistrust, resistance and confusion.

Train, Train, Train

Every January, Kathy, the supervisor, sits down with the child care staff and conducts a training needs assessment for the following year. The goal is to pick topics for forty hours of in-service. At this meeting she also hands out conference brochures and course announcements that she's received from the child care association and the university. During the year she passes out additional information as soon as it arrives.

Continuous training is as important in child and youth care as it is in any other profession. New techniques and approaches are being developed every day. Workers need to keep updated in order to be effective with the children and youth and to make their jobs as easy and enjoyable as possible. Following are a few of the guidelines followed in modern in-service programs.

Conduct a Needs Assessment:

Effective in-service programs begin with a needs assessment to determine which areas of training seem most vital to the participants. Individual interviews, questionnaires asking workers to rank order topics, and group priority setting sessions are just a few of the needs assessment processes which are being used.

Forty Hours is Only a Minimum:

In several states, forty hours of in-service training per year in addition to the initial introductory forty hours are required for group care agencies. This is just a start. In most cases, several more hours are needed.

Combine Inside and Outside Training:

Workers need agency specific training as well as training from the outside. Inside training can be geared to specific cases and problem solving situations. Outside training (conferences, workshops, courses, etc.) offers new insights and a broader understanding of the field.

Train the Trainers:

Supervisors who are responsible for training usually have not been hired because of their training skills. If this is the case, then the agency has a responsibility to help the supervisor develop his or her training skills. This can be done by having supervisors attend workshops conducted by experienced trainers and by taking courses in curriculum development and instruction.

Involve Staff Members in Conducting Workshops:

Staff members have valuable information and insights which can enhance the training process. Supervisors can teach workers how to help conduct training sessions. This can improve the quality of training and build worker confidence.

List Objectives:

Every training session should have specific objectives. If time permits, objectives can be determined by needs assessment, the same way that topics were chosen. Following is an example of a training session description and specific objectives.

Workshop
"Discipline Alternatives to Punishment"

This session is designed to introduce workers to long and short term discipline alternatives to punishment. Theory and specific techniques will be presented. Workers will also be given a short self-help quiz to help them identify and develop their own styles of intervention.

Objectives:

Upon completion participants should be able to:
—Identify six characteristics which differentiate effective discipline from punishment.
—Demonstrate five group consequence techniques.
—Demonstrate five individual consequence techniques.
—Demonstrate six time out techniques.
—Demonstrate five restriction techniques.
—Demonstrate nine physical intervention techniques.

—Identify whether they have interactive, non intervention or intervention styles of discipline.

Ninety Minute Minimum:

Most training sessions require adequate time for workers to practice and mull the material over together. Ninety minutes seems like a good minimum with three hours being a good maximum for any single session.

Combine Methods of Instruction:

According to evaluations from dozens of workshops (Child and Youth Care Learning Center, 1986) a combination of formal presentation (e.g., lecture by instructor, guest presenter, films, video tapes, etc.) and group interaction (e.g., role playing, discussion, problem solving, practice, etc.) appears to work best. The objective is to teach a few new concepts or techniques and then let the workers discuss the material and practice techniques.

Evaluate:

Always evaluate sessions to determine if goals and objectives are being accomplished. There are numerous evaluation forms to choose from. (See Appendix A for a sample evaluation form.) Agencies are also increasingly evaluating participants to determine if they have acquired or learned the basic skills being taught. For example, workers are quizzed or asked to demonstrate the techniques for the instructor on video tape. Answers and demonstration are then discussed with the supervisor who points out strengths and weaknesses.

Everyone Deserves an Evaluation

Paul is preparing for his six month evaluation. Like the other workers he must fill out a self evaluation and take it along to two supervisory meetings which will be focused entirely on his performance over the past six months. He and his supervisor have been reviewing his progress towards the goals they set forth together at the last evaluation and so he is not expecting any major surprises. All in all he feels pretty good about how he's done and he's looking forward to a positive evaluation.

Every worker, experienced and inexperienced, needs goals to work towards and objective feedback about whether those goals are being or have been reached. Workers without formal evaluations seem to wander aimlessly through their jobs, never quite certain where they are headed. Workers with a clear direction tend to reach their goals and move on to new ones. Following are a few general guidelines for employee performance evaluations.

Include Workers in Developing the Form:

Workers will try harder to meet general evaluation criteria if they have a part in determining what those criteria should be. Therefore, it is worthwhile to involve workers in discussions about the evaluation process and in developing the instruments which will be used to evaluate them. (There is a sample of an evaluation form developed by a team of workers in the Appendix at the end of the book.)

Self Evaluations:

It is helpful if workers do a self evaluation before coming to their formal evaluation. This allows the evaluator and the worker to identify differences and similarities in perception.

A Continuous Process:

Goals and objectives should be set together (supervisor and worker) and reviewed throughout the year. When evaluations are an ongoing process, workers are rarely surprised at their next formal evaluation and they are more likely to be on target in reaching their goals.

Team Evaluations:

Effective team members are able to evaluate each other. On some treatment teams, team members fill out and then discuss evaluations with each other. The supervisor or team leader is responsible for the final evaluation but he or she listens carefully to team recommendations and encourages team members to conduct constructive evaluations of one another. Properly conducted team and individual evaluations are usually a positive learning experience for everyone involved.

Proposals for Change

Ken has been working on his proposal for a step plan for almost two months. Next week he plans to add the finishing touches and submit it to his supervisor. In the proposal he's included two major reasons why he thinks an incentive system will improve the agency. First, over the long run he thinks it will provide the support

*that's needed to keep the most effective workers.
And nothing is more important to the kids and
their ability to develop relationships than having
committed, experienced staff members. Right now,
for example, he thinks at least five other top
workers would be willing to stay for another two
years if they were given the proper incentive. No
one wants to leave, but it's getting pretty hard to
survive on current salaries.*

*Second, Ken thinks a step plan will save money
over the long run. He's done his homework and
found out that the agency spent a lot on absenteeism and turnover during the past year, almost
enough to pay for another position. His premise,
based on some studies he's read, is that these costs
can be cut back by providing greater incentive
for workers to stay. This saving, along with the
4% increase the state has approved in it's rates
for next year, should more than finance his proposal.*

Some workers may remark that "It's nice to
know that these things will make us more happy
and effective in our work, but if we don't have
them how can we ever get them?" If you are in
this group, the answer is to get involved like Ken
in making constructive proposals for change. Don't
wait for others to do it for you. There are two
reasons to take action. First, no one knows your
needs better than you do. Second, others can't be
expected to pursue your goals with the same
intensity as you can.

Following are a few tips to follow while developing proposals for change.

Base It on the Children's Needs First:

One of the advantages of being a worker is that
you are in a position where you can get to know

the youth and their treatment needs better than anyone else. This knowledge can be used as the foundation for a successful proposal. In other words, if a proposal for a schedule change, a training program or a step plan is being made, it will be strengthened by your awareness of how this change will improve the quality of care for the youth. Proposals that do not attempt to improve the quality of life for youth should not be made.

Look for a Precedent:

Most changes have a precedent someplace. This is hard to believe sometimes, especially for workers who are isolated, but workers who do their homework at the library and who talk with workers outside the agency at association meetings and conferences know that there are usually plenty of examples to be found. For instance, the suggestions in this chapter are all based on actual programs which are in place at child and youth care agencies. Hence, it pays to get out and look around.

Know your Facts Inside and Out:

Sound proposals are supported with data or facts. General facts can often be found in research studies and in conversations with outside professionals. This information can then be integrated into the proposal. For example, "In a recent study of child care workers it was found that weekly supervision was considered to be one of the most important elements in their development." Specific facts can be found in treatment planning documents, log notes and your own observations of the youth and colleagues. For example, "Without double coverage on Sunday nights we've had twice the number of incidents as on nights with double coverage." Or, "Six of the last seven workers who left said it was because there was not a chance to advance within the agency."

It is also important to know the facts about how the agency is influenced from the outside. For example, "Last year the legislature approved a six percent salary increase, but it did not put any restrictions on how the money should be distributed." Or, "Last year we spent almost $10,000 on overtime because we needed people to cover for turnover."

Work Together:

Proposals developed by study groups or committees have more clout than proposals developed by individuals. Often an individual has to take the initiative to get things going, but it shouldn't be long before he or she solicits the support of others and, whenever possible, the approval of administration.

Avoid "We/They" Struggles:

Proactive proposals are designed to inform, share, and recommend, not to alienate or prove others wrong. Workers who go into it as if they are at war usually lose the battle.

Be Ready to Compromise:

As in many treatment decisions, proposal developers have to be prepared to compromise. Proposals are rarely accepted as is.

Try Again:

If the proposal fails, try again later with a different strategy. Sometimes it takes two, three, even four attempts to find the right combination.

Summary

In this chapter several organizational practices which appear to increase worker satisfaction were presented. The objectives were to: a) provide students and other job candidates with information that will help them in making an initial job choice, b) encourage workers and administrators to review their current recruitment, decision-making, administrative, supervisory, scheduling, and evaluation policies in light of this information and to adapt their policies accordingly, and c) stimulate more interest in the effort to better understand how these and other organizational factors promote satisfaction and stability.

Chapter Two References

Baker, E.A. (1976) Symposium: Supervising child care personnel. *Child Care Quarterly,* 5,(1).

Child and Youth Care Learning Center (1986) Summary of workshop evaluation forms. Unpublished.

Fleischer, B. (1985) Identification of strategies to reduce turnover among child care workers. *Child Care Quarterly,* 14, (2), 130-139.

Freudenberger, H.J. (1977) Burnout: Occupational hazard of the child care worker. *Child Care Quarterly,* 6, (2).

Katz, D., and Kahn, R. (1978) *The social psychology of organizational behavior.* New York: John Wiley and Sons.

Krueger, M. (1983) *Careless to caring for troubled youth.* Milwaukee: Tall Publishing.

Krueger, M. (1985) Job satisfaction and organizational commitment among child and youth care workers. *Journal of Child Care,* 2, (3), 16-24.

Krueger, M., Lauerman, R., Grapham, M., and Powell, N. (1986) Characteristics and organizational commitment of child and youth care workers. *Child Care Quarterly,* 14, (1).

Krueger, M., Lauerman, R., Savicki, V., Parry, P., and Powell, N. (1987) Characteristics of child and youth care workers: A follow up survey. Forthcoming in *Journal of Child and Youth Care Work.*

Krueger, M., and Nardine, F. (1984) The Wisconsin child care worker survey. *Child Care Quarterly,* 13, (1).

Mattingly, M. (1977) Sources of stress and burnout in professional child care work. *Child Care Quarterly,* 6, (2).

Porter, L., and Steers, R. (1978) Organizational work and personal factors in employee turnover and absenteeism. *Psychological Bulletin,* 80, 151-176.

Porter, L., Steers, R., Boulion, P., and Monday, R. (1974) Organizational commitment, job satisfaction, and turnover among psychiatric technicians. *Journal of Applied Psychology,* 59, 151-176.

Rosenfeld, G. (1978) Turnover among child care workers. *Child Care Quarterly,* 8, (1).

Ross, A. A study of child care turnover. *Child Care Quarterly,* 13, (3), 209-224.

Vander Ven, K., and Thompson, C. (1986) International directory of training and educational programs in child and youth care practice. In Press.

CHAPTER THREE:
TEAMS

Teamwork has become a way of life at Lake-view. The workers willingly accept the fact that their interventions with the kids have to be based on the decisions they make together as team members. Every Tuesday and Thursday after-noon the team—the three child care workers, the teacher, the social worker and sometimes the kids and their parents—sit down together to "process" their feelings and to plan. It's tough work. There are differences of opinion, pressures to get a lot done in a short period of time, and difficult com-promises. But it is also rewarding. At some meet-ings, team members really seem to click: they support one another, discover exciting alterna-tives and leave rejuvenated for the next shift. In the final analysis, if you ask each of the team members if it was worth it, they'd all probably give a strong yes.

The team model is the most popular method of treatment decision-making and delivery in youth work today (Garner, 1980; Krueger, 1986; Vander Ven, 1979). Practitioners and administrators alike seem to be sold on teams. Why? Because after several years of experience and study (Brendtro and Ness, 1984; Fulcher, 1981; Garner, 1982; Krueger, 1982; Vorrath and Brendtro, 1974), most people in the field believe that teamwork promotes worker satisfaction and effectiveness. In other words, the popular notion is that if the doors are opened for workers to be involved with one another in developing and implementing treatment plans, desirable outcomes will be created for them and the youth they serve.

Yet, while teams are enjoying tremendous popularity, even the strongest supporters will admit, "It isn't easy." In a recent study of eight treatment teams it was discovered that team members were having difficulty implementing teams according to their own designs (Krueger, 1982). Unresolved issues in departments representing teams (Garner, 1980), administrative reluctance to grant workers equal professional status (Vander Ven, 1979) and lack of time and resources have also been identified as major deterents to teamwork. Add to this the job stress which is inevitable when workers must confront, assert and compromise and it becomes apparent why some people struggle more than grow with teams.

Nonetheless, most of us who have had a chance to experience several years of teamwork are more convinced than ever that teams hold the key. There is perhaps no more meaningful work experience than to be able to be part of a team of people who are working and growing together as they attempt to improve the quality of care for youth. The positive support, constructive criticism, cohesiveness, and creativity, which can flourish on effective teams, simply can't be duplicated in any other way.

In this chapter, therefore, we will devote time to making the team experience more productive. Specifically, we will look at a few of the structural and human conditions which seem to contribute to making teams conveyors of satisfaction and treatment effectiveness.

Definitions:

Teams—Two or more individuals who are assigned to work with one or more youth and their families. For example, teams can consist of two foster parents or several staff members from various disciplines (e.g., a social worker, three child care workers, a teacher, and an administrator). Children and parents also play a significant role on many teams.

Teamwork—A process in which team members convene on a regular basis to design and implement individual treatment plans for a specific group of youth.

Consensus—A majority vote in which members of the minority agree to compromise and implement the approach or technique being discussed.

Structural Ingredients

Teams need a foundation or structure on which to operate. The human conditions that team members bring to the teamwork process need a strong base of support. For example, holding team meetings requires a workable meeting schedule and some procedures to govern behavior during meetings. In this section, therefore, we will begin by looking at some of the structural ingredients for implementing teams. Many of the suggestions presented here are based on recommendations from an implementation study of eight treatment teams (Krueger, 1982). The objectives are to describe a few effective team policies and procedures, and to set the foundation for the next section where we will look at some of the human interactions that are at the crux of the team process.

Two important facets of team development, leadership and mutual adaptability are emphasized in the following vignettes and recommendations. While teamwork is based on decentralized management units, leadership is still central to implementing and guiding these units; someone has to be in charge. With effective leadership in place, teamwork then becomes dependent on the ability of staff and administrative policies to constantly adapt to changing conditions.

Getting Started

Carl, in his new role as director of the Hilldale treatment complex, wants to put most of his energy into helping teams run better. He feels that all the teams, those in the residential sector, the group home sector, and the community sector, need to reevaluate and get back on the right track. So he begins by setting a schedule of meeting dates in which all of the staff will have a chance to contribute to a planning process. At these meetings members will be expected to identify strengths and weaknesses of their teams and prepare to redefine them accordingly. Carl expects that the outcome will be a new agency team philosophy.

"Bad start" team agencies are characterized by apathy and a lack of feeling of ownership in the team process. In these agencies teams may have been operating for years but when team members are asked to define teams or the team philosophy, they struggle for an answer. And needless to say, it is difficult to enjoy and use a mode of transportation if you're not sure how it's supposed to run.

So, whether working in a new or old team agency, it is important for everyone to be familiar with team definitions and philosophies. One of the best ways to make sure this happens is to periodically involve the entire staff in revising and updating team policies. In addition to staff discussions, surveys and interviews can be used to gather information about teams. The objectives are to get as much input as possible, to give full time ownership to the staff by involving them in designing and shaping the model, and to make sure that policies are reflective of current needs. In this context, final definitions, philosophies and policies are only as important as the process itself.

The overall goal is to design teams in such a way as to permit the workers to effectively integrate the agency philosophy of care and treatment into individual treatment plans for youth. Of course, if an agency does not have a philosophy of care and treatment, then it would be wise to develop a philosophy statement first.

A Written Plan of Attack

After the staff members have had several planning meetings and the chance to modify their role definitions, the structure of teams, and the team assignments, Carl instructs them to write down their objectives and strategies for implementing teams in a similar fashion to the way they write objectives for their treatment plans. Team A writes: "In six months we will be meeting for two hours at least twice a week," "Two self assessment inventories will be completed by March 1st," and "All team members will have completed the workshop in teamwork and communication by March 1st."

Team members who share a clear understanding of the design and long and short range plans for implementing their teams are going to work together better than team members who do not. "Wheel spinning," for instance, is commonplace on poorly defined teams; on the other hand team members who know where they're headed usually reach their destination. The goal is to give teams the same type of attention that we give to the goals and objectives in the youth's treatment plans. We can't be accountable to the youth if we aren't accountable to ourselves.

Who Makes What Decisions

Next Carl explains to the staff that there are certain decisions only he can make. He says, "For instance, I feel I must have the final say on budgets, intakes and discharges. I will weigh your recommendations heavily in making my decisions, but at this point I must take final responsibility in these areas. My goal for the future is to turn many of these decisions over to you. In the meantime I promise to be open about my reasons for all of my decisions and I will share as much information as I can beforehand. This will help prepare you to make these decisions in the future."

A clear understanding of who has what decision-making authority is as important as the ability to shift decision-making responsibility to teams. Ideally, teams will make many of the management and treatment decisions, and their decisions will be based on the identified needs of the children. All teams, however, are in different stages of development and often important decisions must remain in the hands of experienced administrators. There are also some major decisions which only administrators can make. The objective then is to be as clear as possible about the lines of decision-making authority and any plans for altering or changing these lines. It is also important for administrators to explain why they must make certain decisions and the reasons for their decisions. Team members often become disgruntled and teams ineffective in environments where the lines are blurred. On the other hand, team members tend to be very cooperative in environments where they understand how much authority they have and the reasons others are making decisions that impact on their ability to treat the youth.

Move Away From Departments

After the new teams have been in operation for a few months, Carl informs his social work, education, and child care department heads that he wants them to consider eliminating their departments and allowing teams to more or less function as independent treatment units. This would mean that the heads would be responsible for supervising interdisciplinary team members, instead of just social workers, child care workers or teachers. They would also be responsible for helping the team self supervise and for helping members of the various disciplines work more closely together as equal members of a team. Carl's feeling is that this approach will eliminate many of the unresolved intra-departmental issues that have been interfering with team decision-making and free team members to concentrate their energies on what is best for the total child as opposed to their special areas of professional interest.

Teamwork Primacy (Brendtdo and Ness, 1984), Total Team (Garner, 1982) and Generic Team (Krueger, 1983) advocates believe that traditional departmentalization (assigning staff members to departments according to their professional or occupational affiliation) often interferes with team functioning. According to their studies, departmentalization is responsible for creating competitive situations in which departments struggle to protect their special social work, education, child care, etc. piece of the youth and for placing team members in a situation where they are torn by having "one foot in a department and another on a team" (Garner, 1980), often with different sets of rules and interests for each. This in turn has "set up" team members to waste energy in resolving departmental issues rather than concentrating on what is best for the youth. For instance, departments often have different philosophies about issues such as discipline, structure, and even treatment which tend to get played out in team meetings (Krueger, 1982).

Proponents of Total Team, Teamwork Primacy and Generic Teamwork have found that without departments, teams seem to be able to concentrate more on their own needs and the needs of the children (Krueger, Fox and Friedman, 1986). Hence, it seems reasonable for more agencies to move in this direction.

If eliminating departments is not feasible, then department heads might have to focus more attention on how they function as a team. Important factors in this regard are that each department head has an equal position of authority in the organizational structure and that department heads are striving for consensus decisions. If leaders are working in harmony, then teams are more likely to follow their beat.

Equal Recognition

Convinced that Total Teamwork is the answer, Carl and his department heads, now team supervisors, begin holding discussions about how they can promote equal status among team members. They realize that if they are encouraging team members to be equally involved in decision-making, they must also be willing to provide appropriate incentives and leadership opportunities. So they begin to explore how training, salary structures, leadership tracks and meeting schedules can be balanced more fairly for all team members.

Agencies are notorious for inviting child and youth care workers to join in a shared team decision-making process and then continuing to pay them far less than other team members, keeping the doors to leadership positions closed, ignoring their training needs (particularly in teamwork and communication), and scheduling team meetings on their days off or "while they're with the kids." The switch to teams involves tough choices and one of the toughest is making a commitment to drawing workers' status more in line with the status of team members with social work and backgrounds in education. This can be done. For instance, there are programs in which all team members, regardless of educational or professional background, are hired into the same salary structure, trained together for equal amounts of time, given the same chance to become team leaders, and scheduled to attend an equal number of team meetings (Krueger, Fox and Friedman, 1986). This requires some readjustment on the part of those who formerly had more status than others and more emphasis on hiring child and youth care workers with preservice training and good team skills, but over the long run it appears to be both cost and treatment effective (Krueger, et. al., 1986). In other words, when barriers created by arbitrarily awarding greater status to a few team members are removed and individuals are allowed to learn, grow, and share on an equal basis, they tend to work with, rather than against one another.

A Clear Decision-Making Process

At a full staff meeting, Carl says, "We need to take more time to be sure that everyone is involved and agrees with our final decisions. I've been observing teams and I find that important issues are often glanced over with the assumption that everyone agrees. Then when I observe people in action, I feel that they sometimes tend to do their own thing as opposed to what had been agreed upon. Now does anyone have any suggestions?"

Consensus building is hard work. Some agencies simply give up or refuse to get involved in team decision-making because it's simpler to have one person in charge. But if an agency and its members truly believe in teamwork then they have to be willing to work at it. Decisions have to be made with the assurance that people do in fact agree. This often requires compromise, further discussion and exploring alternatives until true consensus is reached. Casual nods of the head and assumptions are not adequate. Feelings have to be "checked out," and an effort has to be made to make sure everyone is ready to act in harmony. This is sometimes a painstaking process, but with practice and perserverance it does pay off. One way to work on this is to make sure each team member comments and gives a definite no or yes with each major decision.

Promote Teams Outside The Agency

Proud of his agency's investment in the team process, Carl begins to talk about his teams with people outside the agency. He "talks it up," at the meeting of association directors, invites parents and people in the local community to come in and meet the staff, makes phone calls, and sends brochures to purchasers of service and state officials.

When you're convinced that you've found something that can work and you're trying hard to do the best you can, it's important to share your enthusiasm and success with people outside the agency. Their support and understanding are very important to implementing teams. For example, placement agencies that understand and accept an agency's particular team concept are more likely to refer clients to them and to support the treatment decisions of team members. Like the plans team members develop for children, teams must be implemented systemically through both internal and external systems.

Make Them Permanent

At six months, after a sufficient period of trial and error, Carl gives all the staff members a draft of the agency's team philosophy, the role definitions of team members, the operating procedures

*for teams, and team evaluation forms. In his
cover memo he asks everyone to study the material and come to the next staff meeting prepared
to contribute to a final draft which will represent
agency policy for the next year.*

If teams are indeed the central decision-making
and delivery approach, written policies usually
reflect this. Searches of file cabinets will be rewarded
with updated team documents and conversations
with team members will reveal a keen awareness
of what has been filed away. Administrators and
practitioners who are really sold on teams seem
to understand that evaluation and documentation
are as essential to success as other elements of
implementation.

Human Conditions

With the proper structural ingredients in place,
efforts can be focused on enhancing the human
condition, the processes and interactions that occur
among team members as they work together. This
is where the action is; the place where people test
their skills and try to constructively criticize and
support one another. Following are a few examples of the dynamics and approaches that seem
central to understanding and working with the
human condition.

Support

*John and Max are sitting next to each other in
the conference room waiting for the team meeting to begin. "John, I was really impressed by the
way you handled the group last night. When you*

get some time, will you give me a few tips," Max
says.

"Sure, but you've been doing pretty good your-
self, for a rookie that is. Ha. Seriously, I think
you're catching on pretty fast," John responds.

Then Margarette, the team leader, asks for their
attention and starts the meeting, "First of all I
want to thank you all for the extra work you put
in on the Thanksgiving ceremony. The kids got a
lot from it. I also want to tell you how good I
feel about the way we seem to be communicating
with each other these days. . ."

Support is needed from fellow team members
to fill the missing void from the outside, to ease
the stress, to promote growth over stagnation, and
to create an environment in which team members
can be open with each other, confront one another,
and criticize each other in a productive way. Without it, things deteriorate very quickly. With it team
members can grow together.

Most team members recognize the need for support. Yet, the nature of the work also makes it easy
to get caught up in the "pathology" or the nega-
tivity that is abundant in the lives of disturbed,
troubled youths and in the attitudes of insensitive
outsiders who don't fully understand the difficult
nature of the work. When this happens team members tend to see weaknesses as opposed to strengths,
faults instead of positive qualities, and so on. In
order to keep this from happening, support has to
be consciously built into the daily agenda. Team
members have to seize every opportunity that they
can to pat one another on the back for a job well
done and to encourage each other to pursue an
alternative course when the present one is failing.
Beginning team meetings and informal interac-

tions on a positive note and setting specific time aside during meetings and in supervisory sessions to point out individual strengths are a couple of strategies that seem to work.

Sharing Resources

For next Thursday's in-service session, Nick, a youth worker, is scheduled to do a presentation on therapeutic recreation. The following week, Nancy, the teacher, will be doing something on learning disabilities.

Having an opportunity to teach and learn from one another is one of the most rewarding experiences in teamwork. Everyone likes to know that they have something of value which can be taught to others and learning often seems much more meaningful when it is done with someone who has worked with the kids. Teams that don't provide an environment in which team members can share their resources are missing the boat completely.

Time to Process

"O.K. gang," Mary, the team leader says. "Let's stop a minute and see where everyone is at. It feels to me like some of us are a little angry or perhaps frustrated."

Like the youth, team members often become frustrated and angry with each other. Disagreements, time pressures, different individual agendas for meetings, and personality clashes are just a few of the conflicts that arise whenever people must work closely together. The feelings that are evoked in trying to resolve these conflicts can't be ignored. People need time to talk about and process their feelings; to explore why they're upset or tired so that they can reduce the tension and move forward.

Unfortunately, however, team members often avoid the need to process. When this happens, whatever the reason—time, fear of confrontation, unwillingness to be open etc., it is difficult to problem solve. With feelings left unrecognized, team members tend to dig in, resist and stop communicating, if not overtly, then covertly.

Some teams build in regular times to meet which are devoted entirely to giving team members a chance to discuss their feelings about one another and any other issue associated with team development. Another common strategy is to stop the meeting (usually for a set period of time) whenever a team member requests time to process. The important factors seem to be that time is set aside and that this time is used exclusively to discuss feelings, always remembering that the way adults support and confront one another is usually reflective of the way they will work with kids.

Territoriality:

It's been two weeks since John, the team leader, asked for child care volunteers to work with the team teacher in the classroom. And he still hasn't had any takers. This bothers him because it isn't the first time team members have failed to volunteer to try something new. Reluctant to assign someone to the classrooms, he calls a special meeting of the workers to discuss why there haven't been any volunteers.

Effective teamwork promotes the development of human resources and challenges participants to expand their horizons. This is precisely what is so enticing to the energetic, creative workers who commit themselves to teams. Yet, taking on new ground is not always as simple as it may seem. It is said that man is by nature territorial. We all seem to have a need to protect what we have and stick with what is familiar. Wanting to grow, change, and take on additional responsibilities is one thing; doing it is another, especially in a demanding, already stress filled, child and youth care environment. Rather than fight territorial instincts, however, it seems best to recognize them and then attempt to widen boundaries according to abilities. Team members and leaders can facilitate this process by reminding and encouraging each other in a supportive, sensitive way; always recognizing that people grow at different rates.

Empathy not Guilt Trips

Things have not been going well for Mac at home. He and his wife are on the verge of divorce. His team members understand this and they are trying to be as sensitive as possible. Bill and Vicki, however, are becoming exhausted because of the extra coverage they've had to provide as a result of Mac calling in sick or simply being unable to come to work. They are also writing some of his reports for him and taking on some of his basic responsibilities such as clothes shopping and distributing allowances.

Empathy, in teamwork as well as in work with youth, is perhaps the single most important human quality. Effective team members strive to put themselves in each other's shoes, to be sensitive to one another's needs. They may not always be able to do it, but they are serious about wanting to be as empathetic as possible. Yet, there seems to be a fine line, which team members often cross, between being empathetic and feeling guilty. And when this line is crossed, good intentions become counterproductive. Team members who lay guilt trips on themselves—start feeling they're not doing enough to help a colleague when they've already done their fair share—can decrease the productivity of at least two people: themselves and the person they are trying to help. Hence, fellow team members and the team leader have to work at trying to be aware of when the line is being crossed. Being empathetic doesn't mean that one person allows another person to be irresponsible nor does it mean that one must absorb another's burden. It is a process in which one strives to understand how another person is feeling while constantly encouraging that person to remain responsible and to perform to his or her capabilities.

Disclosure

"When I was a child my father used to get pretty rough with us, especially before the divorce. I think I'm still pretty bitter about it. I think that's why it's hard for me to accept Maria's parents," Louise says as her teammates listen intently.

Divorce, abuse, chemical dependency or abuse, uneasiness about one's sexuality and other common problems are not isolated among the youth. Many child and youth care workers have been personally touched by these same problems in one way or another. In this regard, they are no different than the general population, but managers and team members often assume or pretend they are not affected. This is a terrible burden to put on the agency and the individuals within an agency.

No one can perform effectively in an environment where personal problems are repressed or denied.

A productive approach is for team members to recognize that they are not immune to the problems and to talk openly about them. If no one on the team is having difficulty then fine. On the other hand, if one or more team members expresses a concern about how they've been influenced by chemicals, abuse, or their parent's sexual attitudes, for instance, then they can work at helping one another. Afterall, this is a helping profession; if we can't help one another then how can we help youth?

If a member is struggling to the point where his or her work is severely effected, then team members might recommend outside help and if necessary encourage the member to leave work until the problem is resolved. In most instances, however, team members can help one another simply by devoting time to recognizing and talking about problems. A further goal is to reach a level of comfort in talking about the problems among themselves so that when they talk with the youth, they are confident and honest with their responses.

Beliefs and Values

"I'm sorry, but I simply can't condone abortion under any circumstances," Jack says.

"But she's only thirteen years old. How can she care for that child" Patty, another member argues.

"I think he needs a little stiffer punishment this time," Todd says.

"Punishment simply is not the answer with these kids. They've been punished enough," Tina responds.

Every team member brings a unique set of beliefs and values to the team. Some of these can be compromised and others can't. This is why it is so important to be thorough during the interviewing process. Team members can't function in an environment where most of their basic beliefs are inconsistent with the prevailing beliefs at their center. On the other hand when belief and value systems are in reasonable sync, team members, with time and support, can find acceptable solutions to many major issues. Once again, team members have to find time to talk and to get to know one another. The objective is to try to understand individual differences and search for common ground in a supportive, respectful fashion.

Authority

"I'm sorry but I can't allow this discussion to continue. You've had sufficient time to arrive at an agreeable working schedule. This time, I'll have to decide. Maybe next time we'll be able to reach a consensus," Marge, the team leaders says.

"Well, if you were going to make the decision all along, why didn't you save us the time?" Tim, a team member, questions. He is sitting with his arms folded across his chest and a rather disgusted look on his face.

"You know that's not fair Tim. We've been trying to work this out together for almost three weeks. We can't go on like this indefinitely. I think your comments are reflective of something else that might be going on between you and me. If they are, I'd like to talk about it," Marge says.

Consensus building and group problem solving are primary functions of teams, but teams also need leaders who are able to exercise their authority when the team is stuck. Sometimes, though, it is difficult to exercise and accept authority, particularly among leaders and team members who are in general young adults in the midst of resolving authority issues in their own lives. It is not uncommon for team members and leaders to test their authority at team meetings. Overreactions and resistance—both passive and active—are fairly common behaviors on teams. This is a normal part of the growth and development of the team and the team members. However, if struggles centered on authority issues are not dealt with, they can be very disruptive to effective team functioning. On effective teams, team members and leaders recognize that the way they deal with and accept authority is important. As in the above example, they also confront one another when the inability to deal with or accept authority is the underlying issue. In supervisory sessions (team and individual) they also discuss feelings and attitudes about authority.

Summary

In this chapter, a few suggestions have been made for implementing teams and for enhancing the human interactions that occur on teams. The premise has been that in order to advance teamwork further, more attention needs to be paid to team policies and greater sensitivity given to the humanness of team members. Administrators and workers are encouraged to discuss the issues presented here and to engage in further study of teams.

Chapter Three References

Brendtro, L., and Ness, A. (1984) *Reeducating troubled youth.* New York: Aldine.

Fulcher, L. (1981) Team functioning in group care. In Ainsworth, F., and Fulcher, L. (Eds.) *Group care for children.* New York: Tavistock. 170-200.

Garner, H. (1977) A trip through bedlam and beyond. *Child Care Quarterly,* 6, (3).

Garner, H. (1980) Administrative behaviors and effective team functioning. *Residential Group Care,* 2, (5).

Garner, H. (1982) *Teamwork in programs for children and youth.* Springfield, Illinois: Charles C. Thomas.

Krueger, M. (1983) Careless to caring for troubled youth. Milwaukee: Tall Publishing.

Krueger, M. (1982) Implementation of a team decision-making model among child care workers. Doctoral Thesis, University of Wisconsin-Milwaukee.

Krueger, M. (1986) Making the team approach work. Forthcoming in *Paedovita.*

Krueger, M., Fox, R., and Friedman, J. (1986) *Implementing a generic team approach: The youth development center.* Submitted for publication.

Vander Ven, K. (1979) Towards maximum effectiveness of a unit team approach: An agenda for team development. *Residential and Community Child Care Administration,* 1, (3) 287-297.

Vorrath, H., and Brendtro, L. (1974) *Positive Peer Culture.* Chicago: Aldine.

CHAPTER FOUR:
CAREERS

Devon, the Director of Human Dimensions, has been in child and youth care for fourteen years. He started as a line worker and, like many new workers, he had a devil of a time his first six to twelve months. The kids really tested him. He jokes about and looks back on that period with fondness now, but he knows that getting through those early months constituted one of the most difficult challenges he's ever faced.

In his second year Devon joined the professional association of workers in his state and began to work on polishing his basic skills. From the very first day he liked the kids and his fellow team members, but now he found additional rewards in being able to talk about his work with other workers at association meetings.

The next two years were years of tremendous growth. He became leader of his treatment team and began work on a master's in Educational Psychology with a special focus on child and youth care. By then, he'd already decided that his goal was to develop a career in the field. He knew it would be tough, but he'd met several other career workers in the association so he knew it could be done. Developing his leadership skills on his team and getting a master's were two major steps toward his goal.

During his sixth year he completed his master's and took over as the child and youth care super-

visor, a position he held for two years until he became director of child and youth care. He also served one term as president of the association and one term as a state delegate to the national child and youth care worker organization. While working on a project for the national organization, he met two workers with a similar interest in group work and they wrote an article together which was published in a national journal.

In his third year as director of child and youth care, Devon got an idea for a model group home program for aggressive disturbed youth. After thinking it through very carefully, he developed a proposal for "Human Dimensions" by basing it on his teamwork and child care experiences. Five months later the county accepted his proposal and he was hired as the director. Now he is still serving as director of a model program he developed five years ago. When his friend who'd left child and youth care to become a social worker asked him if he was pleased with his career decision, Devon said, "Wouldn't trade it for a career in any other field."

Some optimists, the author included, feel that for people like Devon, youth care is an excellent human service profession in which to build a career. Our enthusiasm comes from having found fulfilling careers for ourselves and from our confidence that child and youth care is an emerging profession in which more and more career doors are being opened.

Others feel the opposite. They tend to see child and youth care as a dead end profession, a place where people spend short periods of time while they look for something more profitable to do.

These widely varying opinions, no doubt, confuse many workers who are trying to decide whether or not to stay in the field. Unfortunately, there is no simple anwser. Both opinions are correct. Child and youth care is increasingly becoming a field in which committed, creative, ambitious, assertive workers can build a fulfilling career, but it is also still just another job or a stepping stone for many. This chapter is directed at the first group, individuals who like the work and who want to work hard at carving a career in an emerging profession. In the process we will also try to convince some of the "fence sitters" to start a career as well. The chapter includes a discussion of five career tracks, several career enhancing activities, and eleven steps for building a career in the field.

Tracks and Enhancers

For years, many child and youth care professionals felt front line workers were the only legitimate child and youth care workers. Fortunately, this thinking has now become rather archaic. In 1977, Jerome Beker, Editor of *Child Care Quarterly,* cautioned those who held on to this old notion by stating, "If we continue to maintain, as many of us have, that promotions somehow taint the 'purity' of the child care worker, we will never attain professional status" (Beker, 1977, p. 166). He was suggesting that child and youth care, like other professions, needed to create positions and make room for child care educators, administrators, researchers, etc. in order to gain both influence and legitimacy. Evidently his words and those of other visonaries have hit home: in the most recent survey of workers, 30% of the respondents who identified themselves as child and youth care professionals indicated that their primary role was either administration, supervision, education and training or "other" (Krueger, et. al., 1987).

Thus, today there do indeed appear to be at least five tracks which workers with long term career aspirations can pursue—Direct Service, Administration, Program Development, Education, and Research and Writing. In each track there are also dozens of career enhancing activities (enhancers). Following is a description of the tracks and several enhancers.

Direct Service

Bob has always seen himself as a direct line worker and his agency is glad he has. They want to keep him and other good workers on the line as long as they can. That's why they have a step plan. Bob, of course, has worked hard to meet the criteria in each category and now, in his sixth year, is working toward becoming a youth worker IV. The pay and benefits at this level aren't great, but they are sufficient to get by on. Bob is also making additional money by conducting workshops in recreation at some of the other agencies.

Direct service is where child care professionals begin and where many hopefully want to stay. It is the meat of the profession. Up until a few years ago, however, it was almost impossible for creative, energetic workers to remain in direct service for more than a few years. They simply could not survive on the salaries that were offered and under working conditions which were unrealistically demanding. Now, in at least some agencies, this has changed. Fifty-three percent of workers are in agencies with step plans (Krueger, et. al., 1986). With the advent of step plans, teams, and more favorable working conditions and environments, workers can plan to stay in direct service for longer periods of time. Whether sufficient numbers will be able to remain in direct service for their full careers is still debatable, but it does seem to be a more realistic option for people who'd like to stay for five to ten years, that is, if they "shop around" and find the type of place that will support their career plans (more about this in the next section).

Direct service is also a primary career enhancer for each of the remaining tracks. In other words, it is almost impossible to be effective in other areas of child and youth care without a good, fairly lengthly, direct service experience. In turn, workers who choose to stay in direct service can and are augmenting their direct service careers by taking advantage of opportunities to write, conduct research, and teach.

Administration

Jack recently became executive director of a Home and Community service program. He'd worked almost ten years as a supervisor and front line worker before he applied for the job. He'd also gotten a degree in administrative leadership. When he applied, the screening committee was impressed by his insights about children. Under the old executive director, a social worker, they rarely got such vivid accounts of day-to-day events. They were also impressed by Jack's ability to assess the relationships between budgets, buildings, and treatment.

Jack is typical of an increasing number of workers who are moving into administration after a successful direct line experience. They seem to bring with them a good balance of practical knowledge of the ins and outs of caring for kids and the necessary emotional fortitude and discipline required to make tough decisions. They also tend to operate programs in which workers receive a fair share of the agency resources.

Program Development:

Feeling that her skills could be better used if she were able to employ them in the youths' homes, rather than in the treatment center in which she had worked for ten years, Tina decided to develop an "in home program." "I'll go into the homes and help the parents manage their children. My colleagues and I will be there at mealtimes and bedtimes, whenever we can help resolve a crisis or teach the parents how to enjoy the children. That's one of the major problems, you know. They don't know how to parent, how to have fun. And who knows more about parenting troubled kids than we do?" she said as she tried her proposal out on a couple of fellow workers.

"I think I can operate an effective group home with a team of experienced, decently paid workers. If the county will give us a chance, I think I can show them that youth workers can run a program that is cost effective and treatment effective without all the unnecessary support services and red tape," Tom, a youth worker with

five years experience, said to his colleagues at an association meeting.

Pie in the sky ideas? Absolutely not. These are precisely the kinds of ideas that more and more workers are putting into practice in programs which they have developed. Keenly aware that child and youth care holds many of the cost and treatment effective solutions to youths' problems, they are finding creative new ways to use the skills and knowledge they developed on the line. For example, in British Columbia, workers contract directly with the government to provide a wide range of youth services. In Wisconsin, a worker has developed her own home and community program and it is receiving accolades from county workers. In Washington, D.C., a worker operates several group homes which are run entirely by youth workers. And in Virginia, a worker has developed a unique team approach for more effective use of his colleagues in a residential center.

Education and Training

Jason has been conducting workshops at association meetings and conferences for almost four years. It was frightening at first—standing in front of a group—but he soon found that his colleagues were very supportive. They understood what it felt like and they appreciated the fresh perspective he had to offer. After his first workshop, one of the participants came up and said, "It's so nice to have an instructor who's been there with the kids." Now he's taking courses in adult education at the U and hoping to teach a course in youth work next semester. He's not sure but he thinks that maybe when he's done

89

with direct line work he'd like to teach child and youth care full-time.

There has been phenomenal growth over the past twenty years in the number and quality of education programs for workers in the U.S. and Canada. For example, in the '60s there were only a handful of formal education programs for workers. Now there are at least three master's, seven bachelor's, dozens of specialties or areas of concentration at the bachelor's level, as well as several two and three year programs (Vander Ven, 1986a). There are also numerous certificate training programs, and international, national, regional, and local conferences. This means that there are many more opportunities to teach than there were before. In the past the few courses and workshops that were available to workers were usually conducted by members of other professions and offered as an adjunct to their own departments and conferences. Today a review of conference brochures and college rosters reveals that many workers have moved into teaching on a part or full-time basis.

Writing and Research

"Jim, you ought to write that program up and send it in for publication," Max, the supervisor said.

"You've got to be kidding. Publishing is for PhDs, not youth workers," Jim said.

"No, I'm not. I heard at a conference that there are at least three journals looking for articles from practitioners. What's the matter? Haven't you read anything lately? Workers are publishing their stuff all the time. Come to my office; I'll show you some journals and newsletters."

There is perhaps nothing more important to the profession than having practitioners make contributions to the child and youth care literature. These contributions are needed to add intensity, practicality, and legitimacy to a body of knowledge which will influence workers for years to come.

Editors of at least three journals *(Child Care Quarterly, Journal of Child Care,* and *Child and Youth Care Work)* have been actively soliciting contributions for the past two years by conducting writers' workshops and publicizing calls for papers. Editors of local and national newsletters are also seeking practitioner pieces for their publications. Even book publishers seem to be showing preference for texts with a practitioner's touch.

In most other fields the competition to get a manuscript published is fierce. In child and youth care editors seem to be begging for articles. Why not give it a try? It can be done. Child and youth care workers are publishing works of all kinds, from technical research (Hunter, 1984) to experiential descriptions of practice techniques (Waggoner, 1984) to essays, poems, and short stories (Waggoner, 1984; Rose, 1985; Schreier, 1986).

While the doors for writing and research are wide open, for most this is not an area that can be pursued as a full time occupation. Few, if any, professional workers are supporting themselves entirely with their writing and/or research. On the other hand, it is an excellent enhancer. Workers who have found time to write and conduct studies can attest to the significant impact a publication or two has had on their careers.

Eleven Steps for Building a Career

We move now to the final section of the book. Appropriately, the objective here is to integrate material from previous sections into a constructive individual plan of action. Following are eleven steps or tips which can help workers and students start to carve out an exciting career in child and youth care.

Get A Good Start

Nancy started looking around for a job in youth work about six months before she graduated. She went to several centers, filled out applications and had about ten interviews. During the interviews she asked questions about the benefits, working conditions, and the treatment philosophy of the agency. The interviewers were impressed by her preparedness and her general knowledge of the field. When she graduated she had two job offers waiting. She picked the one where the interviewers seemed the most open with her and the treatment philosophy most closely matched her own.

Making the correct initial job choice is extremely important to starting a career in the field. The first job is the place where professionals learn the ins and outs of child and youth care. Without a positive initial learning experience it is difficult to grow and advance. Chapters Two and Three include suggestions and recommendations about factors that add to a positive working and learning environment. The objective is to collect as much of this type of information about prospective agencies as possible before accepting the job. This necessitates advance planning and trying to avoid situations where you are pressed into taking a job.

Keep Commitments and Work Hard

There were times in that first year when Sam wanted to leave, but his commitment and the support of his fellow team members kept him going. Other times he was simply too busy learning the job and getting to know the kids. By the start of the second year the work seemed a little easier and he began to feel reasonably competent. He also began to be more assertive in the change process.

For many workers it takes at least a year to feel comfortable coming through the front door every day and two years of practice to learn the basics. Child and youth care grows on professionals as they grow themselves. It can't be learned entirely in a textbook or through brief encounters with youth. It takes time, patience and perserverance.

If a correct choice has been made, there will be opportunities for training, supervision, and teamwork. These are indeed opportunities that should be actively pursued: learning as much as possible at in-service sessions, using the supervisor as a source of support and training, and supporting, cooperating and decision-making with fellow team members. If these opportunities are not available in sufficient doses or if the working conditions need improving, it is never too early to think about a constructive proposal for change. However, be cautious; sometimes the fault lies within. Under the pressures of adapting to a new job, opportunities are often overlooked and conditions exaggerated.

A positive two year performance evaluation is the base on which most careers are built. Mediocrity does not go any further in youth care than in any other professional endeavor. So make the right choice and then work hard to do the best job possible

Start To Know Yourself

"You seem to have a good ear and keen eyes for working with kids," Nancy tells Maria during her supervisory session.

"What do you mean?" Maria asks.

I think that you have the basic qualities of a person who, with some training, could be a good child and youth care clinician. You are fortunate. Not everyone has your ability."

"My team members have said the same thing. I guess I need some help understanding exactly what my strengths are. Will you help me so I can begin to develop some plans for myself."

"Sure, that's what I'm here for," Nancy says with a smile.

Knowing your own strengths and weaknesses is central to making a positive career choice. Like working with kids, however, it takes a conscious, planned effort and it can't be done alone. The advice and insight of fellow team members and supervisors has to be actively sought.

Once specific personal attributes have been identified, they can be paired with the skills needed for a specific track. Karen Vander Ven (1979; 1981; 1984; 1985), a child and youth care professional, has done extensive work in this area. Work such as this, which matches specific stages of development and personal attributes with tracks in the field, is essential reading for career minded workers. This information, combined with the general skills and attributes outlined in Chapter One, and the help of colleagues will aid in a conscious effort to get to know yourself.

Join The Association

Six months after he started work, Jack was approached by Louise, a fellow worker, about joining the state association of child and youth care workers. "What for? What will I get for my fifteen bucks?" he asked.

"You'll get a chance to meet workers from other agencies and to be involved in helping the profession grow," she responded.

Jack looked at her as if to say, That's it? Then he pulled out his wallet and joined, mostly because he didn't want to disappoint Louise.

The benefits of joining a professional association aren't always obvious to newer workers who are engrossed in trying to learn the ropes. They are there, however, and it is never too early to begin. Joining an association creates contacts with other workers who share similar concerns and who are often willing to provide additional support and encouragement. It also provides exposure to the professional world outside the agency. News about job opportunities, educational programs, policies influencing the development of the field and social events is available at meetings and in publications. Not every state has an association, but if this opportunity is available, it is a worthwhile one to pursue. If not, try to attend an association conference in a neighboring state. This will provide similar exposure and perhaps some suggestions for eventually forming an association in your own state.

Choose a Track

"I think I'd like to be an educator some day," Hank says.

"Not me, I'm staying in direct service for as long as I can. That's where the action is," Lanny responds.

"You two can do what you like, but some day I'm going to run this place," Nick says.

This is the type of conversation that is going on among youth workers more and more often. Usually, somewhere during the second year, it is wise to begin thinking about a track around which to mold long term plans. By then an adequate taste for the work and an awareness of various possibilities should have been acquired. This does not necessarily have to be a final decision, but it is important to at least begin to narrow down the possibilities.

Educate Yourself

"How do you do it, Tim?" a friend asks.
"What?"
"Go to school and work full-time?"
"It's hard, but you know I think it actually energizes me. I can relate my studies to my work and it seems to give both more meaning."

If you don't have a bachelor's degree, eventually you'll need one. If you have a bachelor's degree, then it is good to start thinking about a master's in an area that matches the track you've chosen or are thinking about. For example, master's degrees in adult education and administrative leadership are available at most major universities, as are standard courses in counseling. There are also several specific degrees and specialties in child and youth care. So it pays to contact campus recruiters, to attend events such as training conferences, where recruiters are likely to be advertising their programs, and to page through journals (Vander Ven, 1986a). Once an initial adjustment to the job has been made, why delay? Working full time and going to school part time or taking refresher courses is an accepted part of most professionals' lifestyles. Even if plans are not finalized, a course or two won't hurt. Sometimes exposure to a formal learning experience is what's needed to cement a plan together.

Propose Changes

"I have a suggestion," Jill says to her supervisor at the beginning of a team meeting.

"What is it, Jill?"

"Instead of having us work as crisis backup in the morning, why not see if we can't go into the classroom and work alongside the teacher. I'd feel much more productive if I were involved with the guys in a learning experience than I do now waiting for them to misbehave."

"What would we do in the classroom?" another team members asks.

"Tutor, teach high interest and vocational activities, assist the teacher, and run special events."

"Sounds like you've given this a lot of thought?" the supervisor says.

"I have, want to hear my proposal?"

"Yes."

Youth work is an imperfect science; every program has room for improvement. When an imperfection or burdensome condition is in the path of a growing career, make a proposal for change (see

Chapter Two for tips on developing proposals).
Use the communication skills and knowledge that
have been obtained during the first year or two to
initiate change. If a correct choice has been made,
it is usually better to work at creating change at
home, than it is to seek it elsewhere. Workers who
leave for greener pastures often find a set of imper-
fections that are worse than the ones they left
behind.

Make A Second Commitment

*"I'm signin' up for another two," Mike says
jokingly to Bonita after his second annual evaluation.*

*"Good, we need people like you. Besides, now
that you've got your feet wet, you'll finally start
to pay off," She jokes back.*

Once that first commitment has been fulfilled,
most workers will benefit from a second two year
commitment. The second two years are a time to
polish the craft, to take greater risks, and to challenge oneself to find newer and better ways of
working with the youth. It is also a time for being
a bit more objective, perhaps, than at the beginning, when your dreams, aspirations and self
expectations were being tested.

Get Track Experience

*"Bill, I hear you're planning on running for
president of the state child care association. Isn't
that a lot of extra work?" Tim asks.*

*"Yes, but I figure it's a good way to get some
administrative experience. I can learn to work
with a board, handle budgets, lead."*

*"That's right, you want to be an administrator
some day, don't you?"*

Running for office in a professional association, chairing a committee, volunteering to conduct a workshop, going to a public hearing, and writing a description of a technique or a program to circulate among staff members are just a few of the ways that track experience can be obtained. Track experience is work experience which is similar to the type of work you'll eventually be doing in a chosen track. This can occur after a track has been chosen or before. Sometimes it is helpful to get a feel for the work before finalizing plans. Somewhere in the third year, most workers will want to have chosen a specific track.

Get Specific About Education

"I'm glad I took the course in supervision and administration," Bob says.

"Why?" Milt, Bob's coworker asks.

"Now I'm sure I want to complete the administration and supervision track in the master's program."

With two years experience on the line, some track experience, and a course or two under the belt, it's time to get specific about a track (if you haven't already) and education. Usually by the third year, the bachelor's degree should be near completion or the master's started. It doesn't pay to drag it out any longer. Workers who put off going to school or making a choice about a specific area of study beyond this point, often continue to put it off indefinitely. The final educational choice can be made with the help of a child and youth care educator and with the knowledge of your own strengths and weaknesses which you have been cultivating throughout the early part of your career.

Go To It

"You've accomplished a lot in four years, Terry. You've finished your degree, you've made child care worker III, you've developed some terrific relationships with kids and staff, and you've grown personally," the director says as he presents Terry with an award for being the outstanding worker on his team.

"Thanks, Don, but I feel like I'm just beginning."

With sufficient experience and education, it is time to actively pursue the next job. For many this means working towards the next stage in the step plan. For others it may mean a supervisory position or a program directorship. Still others may turn to education.

If the next step is outside the agency, start seriously looking for ads in journals, newsletters, and newspapers for job announcements. Also attend conferences and ask colleagues about potential openings. Let people know you're available. Then go to it. Check out every possibility; even if it isn't exactly what you want. Sometimes employers aren't sure what they want or need until they talk to a creative, energetic child and youth care pro. Give yourself time and whatever you do, don't give up. The opportunities are there for those who have the skill and perserverance to go after them.

Summary

In this final chapter, we have looked at career tracks, enhancers and steps. The objectives have been to provide additional information for professionals who are eager to develop a career plan; to summarize how information from previous chapters can be integrated into a career plan; and to end on a positive note. If after reading this chapter, more workers are excited about building a career in the field, then a major goal will also have been reached.

Chapter Four References

Beker, J. (1977) (editorial) On defining the child care profession. *Child Care Quarterly.* 6, 166.

Ferguson, R., and Anglin, J. (1985) The child care profession: A Vision for the future. *Child Care Quarterly,* 14, (2), 85-102.

Hunter, D.S. (1984) The treatment of an enuretic child in residential care. *Child Care Quarterly,* 12, (4), 321-336.

Krueger, M., Lauerman, R., Graham, M., and Powell, M. (1986) Characteristics and organizational commitment of child and youth care workers. *Child Care Quarterly,* 14, (1).

Krueger, M., Lauerman, R., Savicki, V., Parry, P., and Powell, N. (1987) Characteristics of child and youth care workers: A follow up survey. Forthcoming in *Journal of Child and Youth Care Work.*

Rose, S. (1985) Heart notes from the desk of a child care worker. *Child and Youth Care Work,* 2, (1), 74-75.

Schreier, F. (1986) The death of a child care worker. *Child and Youth Care Work,* 3, (1).

Toigo, R. (1980) Child care—occupation or profession: Searching for clarity. *Child Care Quarterly,* 10, 242-249.

Vander Ven, K. (1984) Life long careers in child care. Presented at International Conference in Group Care. London, May, 1984.

Vander Ven, K. (1981) Patterns of career development in group care. In Ainsworth, F. and Fulcher, L. *Group Care for Children: Concepts and Issues.* London: Tavistock.

Vander Ven, K., and Thompson, C. (1986A) International directory of training and educational programs in child and youth care practice. In Press.

Vander Ven, K. (1986) From child care to developmental life cycle caregiving: A proposal for future growth. *Child and Youth Care Work,* 3 (1).

Waggoner, C. (1984) First Impressions. *Child Care Quarterly,* 12, (4), 247-257.

Waggoner, C. (1984) What to do when the roof is falling, the kids are playing deadman's bluff, the neighbors are at the door, the cops are circling the house and you're in the shower. *Child and Youth Care Work,* 1, (1), 8-16.

Bibliography and Suggested Reading

Baker, E.A. (1976) Symposium: Supervising child care personnel. *Child Care Quarterly,* 5,(1).

Beker, J. (1977) (editorial) On defining the child care profession. *Child Care Quarterly,* 6, 166.

Brendtro, L., and Ness, A. (1984) *Reeducating troubled youth.* New York: Aldine.

Child and Youth Care Learning Center (1986) Summary of workshop evaluation forms. Unpublished.

Conger, J. (1979) *Adolescence and youth: Psychological development in a changing world.* New York: Harper and Row.

Ferguson, R., and Anglin, J. (1985) The child care profession: A Vision for the future. *Child Care Quarterly,* 14, (2), 85-102.

Fleischer, B. (1985) Identification of strategies to reduce turnover among child care workers. *Child Care Quarterly,* 14, (2), 130-139.

Freudenberger, H.J. (1977) Burnout: Occupational hazard of the child care worker. *Child Care Quarterly,* 6, (2).

Fulcher, L. (1981) Team functioning in group care. In Ainswarth, F. and Fulcher, L. (Eds.). *Group care for children.* New York: Tavistock. 170-200.

Garner, H. (1977) A trip through bedlam and beyond. *Child Care Quarterly,* 6, (3).

Garner, H. (1980) Administrative behaviors and effective team functioning. *Residential Group Care,* 2, (5).

Garner, H. (1982) *Teamwork in programs for children and youth.* Springfield, Illinois: Charles C. Thomas.

Hunter, D.S. (1984) The treatment of an enuretic child in residential care. *Child Care Quarterly,* 12, (4), 321-336.

Hylton, L. (1964) *The residential treatment center: Children's programs and costs.* New York: Child Welfare League.

Katz, D., and Kahn, R. (1978) *The social psychology of organizational behavior.* New York: John Wiley and Sons.

Krueger, M. (1983) *Careless to caring for troubled youth.* Milwaukee: Tall Publishing.

Krueger, M. (1982) Implementation of a team decision-making model among child care workers. Doctoral Thesis, University of Wisconsin-Milwaukee.

Krueger, M. (1985) Job satisfaction and organizational commitment among child and youth care workers. *Journal of Child Care,* 2, (3), 16-24.

Krueger, M. (1986) Making the team approach work. Forthcoming in *Paedovita.*

Krueger, M., Fox, R., and Friedman, J. (1986) Implementing a generic team approach: The youth development center. Submitted for publication.

Krueger, M., Lauerman, R., Grapham, M., and Powell, M. (1986) Characteristics and organizational commitment of child and youth care workers. *Child Care Quarterly,* 14, (1).

Krueger, M., Lauerman, R., Savicki, V., Parry, P., and Powell, N. (1987) Characteristics of child and youth care workers: A follow up survey. Forthcoming in *Journal of Child and Youth Care Work.*

104

Krueger, M., and Nardine, F. (1984) The Wisconsin child care worker survey. *Child Care Quarterly,* 13, (1).

Limer, W. Child care training needs assessment. Survey conducted by School of Social Welfare, State University of New York at Albany.

Linton, T. (1971) The educateur model: A theoretical monograph. *Journal of Special Education,* 5, (2).

Maier H. (1979) The core of care: Essential ingredients for children away from home. *Child Care Quarterly,* 8, (3), 161-173.

Mattingly, M. (1977) Sources of stress and burnout in professional child care work. *Child Care Quarterly,* 6, (2).

Myer, J. (1980) An exploratory nationwide survey of child care workers. *Child Care Quarterly,* 9, (1).

Porter, L., Steers, R. (1978) Organizational work and personal factors in employee turnover and absenteeism. *Psychological Bulletin,* 80, 151-176.

Porter, L., Steers, R., Boulion, P., and Monday, R. (1974) Organizational commitment, job satisfaction, and turnover among psychiatric technicians. *Journal of Applied Psychology,* 59, 151-176.

Rose, S. (1985) Heart notes from the desk of a child care worker. *Child and Youth Care Work,* 2, (1), 74-75.

Rosenfeld, G. (1978) Turnover among child care workers. *Child Care Quarterly,* 8, (1).

Ross, A. A study of child care turnover. *Child Care Quarterly,* 13, (3), 209-224.

Schreier, F. (1986) The death of a child care worker. *Child and Youth Care Work,* 3, (1).

Toigo, R. (1980) Child care—occupation or profession: Searching for clarity. *Child Care Quarterly,* 10, 242-249.

Trieschman, A. (1981) *The Anger Within.* (A video tape series). Silver Spring Maryland: NAK Productions.

Trieschman, A., Whittaker, J., and Brendtro, L. (1969) *The other twenty-three hours.* New York: Aldine.

Vander Ven, K. (1984) Life long careers in child care. Presented at International Conference in Group Care. London, May, 1984.

Vander Ven, K. (1979) Towards maximum effectiveness of a unit team approach: An agenda for team development. *Residential and Community Child Care Administration,* 1, (3) 287-297.

Vander Ven, K. (1981) Patterns of career development in group care. In Ainsworth, F. and Fulcher, L. *Group Care for Children: Concepts and Issues.* London: Tavistock.

Vander Ven, K., and Thompson, C. (1986) International directory of training and educational programs in child and youth care practice. In Press.

Vander Ven, K. (1986) From child care to developmental life cycle caregiving: A proposal for future growth. *Child and Youth Care Work,* 3 (1).

Vorrath, H. and Brendtro, L. (1974) *Positive Peer Culture.* Chicago: Aldine.

Waggoner, C. (1984) First Impressions. *Child Care Quarterly,* 12, (4), 247-257.

Waggoner, C. (1984) What to do when the roof is falling, the kids are playing deadman's bluff, the neighbors are at the door, the cops are circling the house and you're in the shower. *Child and Youth Care Work,* 1, (1), 8-16.

Wilson, T., Powell, N., and Winer, T. (1976) The Maryland Association of Child Care Workers Survey.

YOUTH DEVELOPMENT CENTER STAFF EVALUATION FORM*

Ability to Cooperate, Compromise, and Carry-Out Decisions

1. Knows team decisions.
2. Clarifies personal attitudes, feelings and beliefs.
3. Contributes to discussions; offers input and feedback.
4. Displays positive morale.
5. Initiates conflict resolution.
6. Communicates team decisions.

COMMENT:

Rating: 1   2   3   4

Commitment to the Program

1. Speaks positively and objectively about the program.
2. Demonstrates a strong desire to pursue and support treatment goals.

---

* This evaluation form was developed by the child and youth care staff at the Youth Development Center, St. Charles Boys' Home, Milwaukee, Wisconsin.

3. Sustains commitment.

COMMENT:

Rating: 1   2   3   4

Ability to Assess Needs, Plan Activities and Carry-Out Strategies

1. Plans activities on a daily basis.
2. Follows through with assessments.
3. Makes, interprets, and shares observations.
4. Recognizes individual and group planning needs.
5. Displays working knowledge of treatment strategies.
6. Demonstrates originality.

COMMENT:

Rating: 1   2   3   4

Ability to Develop Relationships

1. Demonstrates ability to develop compassion, trust, security, and empathy in relationships.
2. Has awareness of each youth's needs and abilities to personalize interactions.
3. Listens and talks to youth.
4. Shows tolerance and acceptance of youth.
5. Maintains a degree of objectivity.

109

6. Is consistent in interventions.
7. Understands nature of youth/adult relation-ships (authority).
8. Maintains a positive attitude about each youth.
9. Is sincere and honest.

COMMENT:

Rating: 1   2   3   4

Knowledge of Child/Youth Care

1. Understands dynamics of troubled youth and incorporates knowledge into daily interactions with youth.
2. Takes advantage of learning opportunities.
3. Understands various approaches (e.g., Psycho-dynamic, Ecological, Sociological, Behavioral, and Eclectic).
4. Understands and applies YDC treatment phi-losophy.

COMMENT:

Rating: 1   2   3   4

Ability to Demonstrate Oral and Written Communication Skills

1. Is straightforward and concise in communica-tions.

2. Shows congruency between verbal and non-verbal messages.
3. Is able to get ideas across without being misunderstood.
4. Uses communication skills in relationship building.
5. Understands own beliefs and relevancy in effective communication.

COMMENT:

Rating: 1   2   3   4

Ability to Role Model

1. Models behavior targeted in treatment plan and program philosophy.
2. Displays positive attitude toward program.

COMMENT:

Rating: 1   2   3   4

Problem Solving Skills

1. Demonstrates ability to identify and analyze problems.
2. Is willing to compromise.
3. Takes initiative to solve problems.
4. Takes calculated risks in problem solving.

5. Understands difference between individual and group problem solving.
6. Approaches problems in a calm manner.
7. Displays good judgement.
8. Seeks help when stuck.
9. Accepts solutions.
10. Learns from mistakes.

COMMENT:

Rating: 1   2   3   4

Dependability

1. Comes to work on time.
2. Has a good attendance record.
3. Adheres to established policies.
4. Is willing to help in emergencies.
5. Follows through with assignments.
6. Comes to work mentally, emotionally and physically prepared.

COMMENT:

Rating: 1   2   3   4

Ability to be Creative and Flexible

1. Improvises when necessity demands.
2. Has alternative plans.

3. Asks others for new ideas.
4. Explores new ideas.

COMMENT:

Rating: 1   2   3   4

Self Awareness

1. Recognizes strengths and weaknesses.
2. Has realistic self concept.
3. Works on weak points.
4. Knows personal stressors and works to overcome them.

COMMENT:

Rating: 1   2   3   4

Values Clarification

1. Understands own beliefs and value system and how it impacts on work youth.
2. Accepts different value systems without making moral judgements.

COMMENT:

Rating: 1   2   3   4

Ability to Manage Individuals and Groups

1. Uses preventive as opposed to reactive management skills.
2. Displays authority in an "authoritative" manner.
3. Whenever possible, demonstrates the ability to keep individual and group management in balance.
4. Demonstrates self control in stressful situations.
5. Uses appropriate physical control.
6. Uses appropriate time-outs.

COMMENT:

Rating: 1   2   3   4

Leadership

1. Accepts new responsibilities.
2. Knows when to make independent decisions.
3. Keeps team on task.
4. Demonstrates self confidence.
5. Is aware of and willing to step in when needed.
6. Initiates decision-making process.
7. Takes initiative to do what needs to be done.
8. Demonstrates organizational abilities.

9. Delegates responsibility when required.

COMMENT:

Rating: 1   2   3   4

Ability to Develop Special Personal Resources

1. Develops special programs for kids.
2. Shares skills with fellow team members.
3. Pursues new information, ideas and resources in special interest areas.
4. Recognizes personal areas of expertise.
5. Displays enthusiasm for developing special interest areas.

COMMENT:

Rating: 1   2   3   4

WORKSHOP EVALUATION FORM*

Please evaluate the workshop by circling the number which most closely expresses your assessment of each item. Then please explain what led to your assessment in the comment section under each item.

SCALE: 1 = Strongly Disagree
             2 = Disagree
             3 = Agree
             4 = Strongly Agree

1. The material covered in the workshop will be useful in my work.

   Rating: 1   2   3   4

   COMMENT:

2. The material was presented in a clear and understandable fashion.

   Rating: 1   2   3   4

   COMMENT:

---

* This form is used by the Child and Youth Care Learning Center, University of Wisconsin-Milwaukee.

3. The workshop covered both basic and new information.

    Rating: 1   2   3   4

    COMMENT:

4. The presenters were prepared.

    Rating: 1   2   3   4

    COMMENT:

5. The presenters were supportive and sensitive to the needs of the participants.

    Rating: 1   2   3   4

    COMMENT:

6. The presenters held my interest.

    Rating: 1   2   3   4

    COMMENT:

7. There was adequate time for discussion.

    Rating: 1   2   3   4

    COMMENT:

8. All child care workers at our agency should take this workshop.

   Rating: 1   2   3   4
   COMMENT:

9. A follow-up workshop with advanced information should be developed.

   Rating: 1   2   3   4
   COMMENT:

10. I would recommend the following changes in this workshop.

    RECOMMENDATIONS:

                    THANK YOU